The
Blue Piano
and Other Stories

The Blue Piano

and Other Stories

by Carol Montparker

Amadeus Press

Published in 2004 by

Amadeus Press, LLC
512 Newark Pompton Turnpike
Pompton Plains, New Jersey 07444
U.S.A.

Amadeus Press
2 Station Road
Swavesey
Cambridge CB4 5QJ, U.K.

For sales, please contact
NORTH AMERICA

UNITED KINGDOM
AND EUROPE

AMADEUS PRESS, LLC
c/o Hal Leonard Corp.
7777 West Bluemound Road
Milwaukee, Wisconsin 53213 U.S.A.
Tel. 800-637-2852
Fax 414-774-3259

AMADEUS PRESS
2 Station Road
Swavesey, Cambridge, CB4 5QJ, U.K.
Tel. 01954-232959
Fax 01954-206040

E-mail: orders@amadeus press.com
Website: www.amadeuspress.com

Book design by Mulberry Tree Press, Inc.
Printed in the United States of America

Library of Congress Cataloging-in-Publication Data

Montparker, Carol.
   The blue piano and other stories / by Carol Montparker.
      p. cm.
   ISBN 1-57467-087-5
   1. Montparker, Carol. 2. Pianists--United States--Biography. I.
Title.

ML417.M849A3 2004
786.2'092--dc22

2003015794

This book is for Dennis and Kim.

Contents

Contents

Acknowledgements

I AM particularly grateful to a few close and literate friends: Judith Moshan, for endorsing the authenticity of my words, and ferreting out little snags; Beverly Lawn, for her editorial expertise and writer's instincts; and Andrea Klepetar-Fallek, for multilingual checks and moral support. Jacqueline Dee Parker, poet, painter, and writing instructor, offered some invaluable structural suggestions. Howard Schreiber, the son Ernest and I never had together, pianist, writer, attorney, did some fine-tuning with his superb musical and literary ear. Felipe Porto (Solarium Media), my electronics guru, helped me out of some thorny technological jams, thankfully, and created my beautiful website (Montparker.com).

I want to thank Amadeus Press, especially Eve Goodman, for her enthusiasm and belief that these offbeat stories would "work"; and my superb editor, Barbara Norton, who combined the wonderful qualities of patience and understanding with her expertise, delicate touch, and some fine ideas. I am especially thankful to my new publisher, John Cerullo, and talented and meticulous editor, Carol Flannery, not only for their fresh injections of energy and know-how but for their intuitions and kindnesses.

My dear husband, Ernest Taub, facilitates and supports everything I undertake. Beyond value were his corroboration that a story was worth telling, his copy-editing eye that dates back to Harry Taub's printing shop, and above all, the perspective and growth that living with him has given me.

Preface

THESE stories came straight out of a musician's life.

But I found that to be a storyteller, it is sometimes necessary to take a tuck here and there, to cut and paste. Some writers find that exaggeration makes a better tale; in my case, more often I had to tone down the reality, which was stranger than anyone would believe, and I also tampered a bit with the chronology. I believe that the resulting collection of stories together tells a much larger story, a kind of reckoning, much more important than any single episode.

To quote from the foreword to E. B. White's book *The Second Tree from the Corner*:

> Whoever sets pen to paper writes of himself, whether he knows it or not. This, then, is a book of revelations: stories, poems, essays, opinions, out of the past, the present, the future, the city, and the country.

Sometimes my life has seemed like a story a day; but I have periodically struggled with the sense that writing from one's own experience is a vain pursuit, no matter how universally writers have done it. The urge to tell these stories, however, was so compelling that I threw my ambivalence to the wind. When it was necessary, I changed names, left others out, did a bit of weaving and warping, added a dash of fantasy.

A special word about the story "The Island," which seems almost like a fairy tale as I have written it in light of the present-day realities in Haiti. I tried to depict the island country as it was when I was there in the 1970s. Haiti has always been a poor country; but today the abject poverty, indescribable squalor, a series of corrupt governments, their mismanagement, and the consequent withdrawal of foreign aid are considerably worse than what I saw. I will always feel affection and an overwhelming impotence to help Haiti, whose people are beautiful, positive in spirit, courageous, and hopeful when, truly, it all looks so hopeless.

My work on this book had a strong feeling of harvesting; I fished out tales from the past that I'd almost forgotten, while others I could never forget. My files are lighter, but I am far from finished.

There is a time to tell a story. I have left many untold, including some I could never write.

—Carol Montparker

The
Blue Piano
and Other Stories

The Great Pianist

AN old photo tacked to my bulletin board records the great old pianist with his arm around me, puckish smile on his face, uncomfortable frown on mine. That shot had been commandeered by my ex-husband, Rod, who hustled me backstage after a certain memorable concert with the dictum "Anyone who kisses my wife has to submit to a photo!"

Hours earlier I had been lurking like a trespasser in the shadows backstage, surrounded by the pre-concert chaos I know so well; only this was not *my* concert, so I had no real concerns. The musicians were fiddling and tootling fragments from the program, a gorgeous cacophony composed of simultaneous bits of music, like stray puzzle parts, fun to decipher. Stagehands and personnel were flitting around the stage, shifting chairs and stands, and the black, shiny concert grand extended the length of the back wall, waiting until the moment it would be wheeled out onto the apron of the stage for the concerto.

When I met the Great Pianist at a party, several weeks before the concert, he remembered hearing my audition for a piano competition in which I had won honorable mention and took the opportunity to kiss my hand, my cheek, then my other cheek. He asked me whether I would like a ticket to his concert the following month, and I replied that I already had plans to attend with Rod.

"Yes, yes. He will come to the concert, but not to the kissing."

"What kissing?" I had asked, naively. I began to feel half flattered and half flustered by his attentions.

"I'd like you to meet me backstage before the concert and talk to me in the green room."

The maestro wanted to talk to me! I entertained fantasies of it leading to another opportunity to play for him, and to profound discussions about the Brahms D Minor Piano Concerto, which I had performed ten years earlier at age nineteen. My heart beat with excitement at his invitation and I couldn't wait to tell everyone I knew.

I could hear the murmur of the audience in the hall from my dark corner of the wings, a sound that routinely strikes fear and trembling into the hearts and stomachs of performing artists. I recalled that evening backstage when I was to appear as piano soloist in the Brahms concerto. I was sick to my stomach with nerves. My mother was supporting my forehead over the basin in my dressing room as I threw up, praying I wouldn't soil my beautiful strapless robin's-egg-blue taffeta gown. The conductor walked in and asked my mother, "Will she be all right?"

"Yes, yes, just give her a moment." I wasn't certain I would ever get myself out there on the stage, but I did, and the moment I heard that low bass D on the tympani, beginning the long orchestral *tutti,* I knew I'd be fine. It was my best playing, and tonight, ten years later, I felt I could still step in for the maestro at the last moment if anyone needed me to.

A few of the orchestra personnel darted inquisitive glances in my direction, and I was anxious for the maestro to arrive. He finally appeared in a huff, his black greatcoat with its fur shawl collar sweeping behind him, just moments before the conductor was to enter the stage for the opening Beethoven overture. He was furious and shouted at the stagehands to lead him to his dressing room. His driver had arrived late, they had been stuck in traffic, and everyone was to blame. Grumbling his way along the corridor in back of the stage, he spotted me shyly observing him from the shadows and curtly ordered, "You! Come along with me!"

It was not exactly the warm welcome I had hoped for, but at least he had recognized me from the party the month before, even in his enraged state. I had begun to wonder if he would remember his invitation and felt some regret to be there at all; the only comfort was the promise of a rich exchange of ideas about the Brahms.

He closed the door behind us and took off his cloak, arranging it carefully on a hanger. He placed his leather briefcase on the table and took out his music, regarding it with a frown. He removed his tuxedo jacket, folding it across the back of a chair. He gave me not a single glance. The so-called green room was stark white with a bare bulb hanging overhead. I had the fleeting notion that not just lesser-known pianists but even great maestros were consigned to cold, sterile, backstage chambers, in which one listened to one's heart accelerating with the beat of pre-concert tensions.

My thoughts were in disarray and I hardly knew how to comport myself. I opened my mouth to speak, muttering something about the prolonged, beautiful orchestral *tutti,* which could be nerve-racking for the pianist sitting and waiting for the first solo entrance. I whispered some drivel about the piano's role as another orchestral member in this great work and the inevitability of that first piano entrance. The Great Pianist didn't seem to hear anything I said. Suddenly, without any warning at all, he lunged at me, grabbing both my breasts at once with his huge hands, then pushed his face against mine and pressed his old wine-colored lips upon my mouth. I almost fainted. I stepped outside of myself and perceived the surreal scenario: this ancient, wrinkled, pink and white relic of a man I had only ever seen onstage or as a member of a panel of judges, then briefly at a party, was now closer than I could ever have imagined. In my state of vacant shock, through my slitted eyelids, I viewed him, one millimeter away, forcing himself on me. I was repulsed by the flaccidity of his skin, by his sleazy tactics, by my own idiotic naiveté to have believed that I was wanted for my musical or intellectual company. The overture to *Fidelio* was completely audible from the stage, and I imagined a lifelong set of bizarre associations and repulsions that would accompany this beloved Beethoven music whenever I might hear it in the future. To those immortal strains, tiny voices were dialoguing in my head:

"But this is the Great Pianist kissing me!"

"Imbecile! He's using you to stimulate himself. You could be anyone! Don't flatter yourself."

"How could this be happening to me? What do I do?"

"Push him away!"

"How can I push the Great Pianist away?"

But I did manage to wrest myself free from his almost prehensile grip. Although his savage advances probably lasted a total of only one and a half minutes, I was so constricted, I couldn't breathe. I wiped his spittle off my mouth and wanted to run out. Instead I stammered, "I'm sorry. *(What was I sorry about?)* But I thought— we were going to *talk*. I don't know where you—got the idea—." I sounded so childish and stupid to myself, and turned to slink out of the door of the cell. He was clearly done with me, and I fled down the stairs until the applause subsided and I could claim my seat in the audience. My heart was racing at such a frightening pace that I felt it must be quite audible to those around me. Rod looked at me quizzically. What was he thinking about my flushed face? Did he notice I was trembling? Could he guess the little drama I had survived? He was probably thinking I was excited by my backstage encounter. Would I ever be able to tell the whole absurd story to anyone—that I had just witnessed a spectacle in which my musical idol had reduced himself to a swine?

As the concert grand was rolled out, part of me wanted to shout the truth of his character to the entire audience, even as I searched for the means to explain it to myself. I practiced every mind-over-matter exercise I could dream up, trying to sever the reality of his recently revealed vulgarity from the nobility of the music I was about to hear. When the Great Pianist appeared onstage, I tried hard to recapture my former innocent perception of him as the great artist he truly was. His recording of this concerto had been my mother's milk. I had to rescue the hallowed work from damage.

Suddenly I had an epiphany and the ugly episode revealed its meaning to me: it was clear he had used me to distract himself, to excite himself, for his own needs. It was also clear that he thought being the Great Pianist exempted him from conventional codes of behavior. No doubt he had similarly exploited a number of women throughout his career. All of us were tiny instruments, cogs in his perverted process of preparation, and inspirations for his performances. I had thought I knew all there was to know about pre-concert tensions and the fact that each artist must do whatever he or she must do to overcome obstacles and get to a point of complete freedom in order to express. But his preposterous and offensive routine (as seen from my regrettably close vantage point) gave me a few new insights that offered some relief along with a peek at the great human comedy of it all.

All through the long orchestral introduction I threw myself for dear life into the woven strains of the thematic material, as though it were I about to enter as soloist. I knew the masterpiece inside out and allowed myself to move with the music, feeling increasingly calmed and comforted. Then came the moment of the piano's inevitable entrance. His tone and phrasing were seductively beautiful. I was swept mercifully up and into the concerto, away from all harm.

It was a magnificent performance, and when the concert ended and Rod finally asked me about the green room experience, I simply told him that the Great Pianist had kissed me. "That's worth a photo for posterity," he said, and whisked me backstage. I went unwillingly, but passively, to avoid further questions.

The next day, my prevailing emotion was elation at the memory of the beautiful concerto performance; my anger had dissipated and morphed into amusement at the eccentricity of the pianist's "techniques." One or two large questions lingered regarding the emanation of such refined musical pronouncements from such a questionable source, but I could deal with that another time. I was in a delicatessen, and the man at the counter looked at me and said, "Honey, you look like you won the lottery! What happened?"

"Well," I ventured, "did you ever hear of the Great Pianist?"

"No," he replied.

"Never mind."

The Island

I TRIED to imagine how it would be to return to Haiti and conjured up the surreal image of my grand piano against a backdrop of deserted beach. The thought of the beautiful instrument being loaded off a cargo ship onto the docks and through the frenzied Port-au-Prince customs, then bumping along in a truck on dusty roads through the hills of Pétionville until it finally entered the portals of Sergo's colonial mansion made me cringe.

I can remember every detail of my vacation in Haiti with my first husband many years ago, including the moment I met Sergo. Vacations were among the rare times I ever had the chance to paint. Painting is much less physical than playing the piano, makes no demands, has no goals. When I paint I never experience hunger, nor notice the passage of time. The tensions of my life are on hold. I often draw from visual imagery when I play, but when I paint, my head is emptied of everything but the colors, and not even music intrudes itself into the experience. This is something in my life that is pure frivolity, that I can throw away without threatening my identity. I am a musician, not a painter.

I had set up a makeshift easel on the beach, scooped up a container of water, and sponged down the blinding white page in excited anticipation of painting the improvised still life of bougainvillea and hibiscus, propped in my now-empty iced coffee glass. I loaded my brush with brilliant pigment and dropped it into sensuous little pools, letting the paint flow freely through the wetness. The page was aglow with rose madder, cerulean, vermilion, scarlet lake, ultramarine, and I was lost in the sea of dazzling jewel tones.

The spontaneity of the watercolors took me out of myself, as it always did, so that the shadow that suddenly darkened the page startled me.

"Mais que vous êtes douée!" (You are gifted!) The compliment came from a man whom I had noticed earlier; he had looked at me quizzically from his chaise several yards away, then strolled to the water, tall, elegant, with the caramel complexion of a Persian prince. He had an enviably easy and graceful way of moving that seemed to come from an inner confidence and pride. He swam as though he were a creature of the sea, although his presence on that beach seemed exotic, even alien. The soft murmuring quality of his voice, like a berceuse, embodied the mellowness of the island, the balminess of the sea breezes, and the gentleness I felt in the people.

"Thank you. I am enjoying myself, but I am just a holiday painter." Why was I so self-conscious with my French? It seemed so charming when they struggled in English.

But I was also conscious of my flounder-white flesh amidst the *café-au-lait* bodies of the upper-class Haitian women staying at the hotel. Hours earlier I had watched my husband surreptitiously photographing them playing ball. Now, in my two-piece suit, the closest thing to a bikini Rod would "allow" me to wear, I felt uncomfortable.

"Is this your first trip to Haiti?" he asked.

"Yes. Are you a guest here, too?"

"No. I have a home here, but I have been away for many years."

He encouraged me to continue speaking in French, although his English was good. My fears and complexes slowly fell away and we became engaged in an eager exchange of information. He had returned after years of academic life abroad, and his knowledge of music and art were comprehensive. I hadn't expected to have a conversation as rich as that while relaxing on a hotel beach in Haiti. The man was a study in contrasts: an easy grace with a certain formality, statuesque strength with infinite discretion. He possessed a calm that slowly began to envelop me.

Just at that moment Rod returned from his errands. I could see his scowl as he approached.

"Rod, this is Sergo Villefranche. He has just returned to Haiti after fifteen years in Europe."

"Nice to meet you," he mumbled.

"I was just going to offer to be your guide, if you like. It would give me pleasure to show you my island and reacquaint myself at the same time. Then I am sure my mother would be pleased to have you come to our home for lunch tomorrow. Would you like it?"

I could feel Rod's resentment growing. Finally he managed, "Well, I think that would be fine, thank you."

"*Bon.* I will take you in my car. What time shall I come for you?"

"Well, let's say we will meet you in Port-au-Prince. We have some errands to do. Where shall we meet?"

"If you prefer it. The post office at eleven o'clock."

I watched as the man strode across the lawn to his car, hoping he hadn't been offended by Rod's brusqueness, and braced myself for a scene in the room.

The hotel was nestled among the craggy, bald clay-and-lavender colored mountains that had so impressed me from the air. The ecology had long been ravaged by the economy, trees cut mercilessly for fuel and tourist crafts. The only green tropical foliage was near the water. But what Haiti lacked in lush surroundings, it made up in its culture and the beautiful spirit of the people.

I put off going into the bungalow, and went instead to the veranda. Facing the sea, I let my spirit float, and I was infinitely grateful for the sound of Rod's snores from inside the room. At times like these, I asked myself why we never could enjoy anything together. We shared an appreciation for other cultures, and I was grateful for the way he had arranged the entire trip, down to the last detail, with that leave-everything-to-me confidence that first attracted me when I was only seventeen. What I could not anticipate at such a young age was that it was a package deal—it came with his need for total control—and that love, for him, meant possession.

I pondered the ironies and myths that had kept the marriage together way past the point when it had any value to either of us. Rod gave up hopes of a career as a violinist to go into the practical world of business as a means to an end. "Music is more pleasurable as a mistress than to have to be married to it"—he loved the way that explanation rolled off his lips. But he had married me, a nineteen-year-old pianist with a promising career ahead, and had entertained fantasies of our union leading somewhere between heaven and Carnegie Hall. Now he saw himself as a long-suffering commuter who had sacrificed his dreams. I secretly believed his dreams were unrealistic, yet we continued to perform together, mostly in smaller halls near our home. I felt both grateful and guilty for the material comforts that Rod had been providing while I continued to pursue my solo concert work and teaching. I made sure I did all of my solo practicing when he was out for fear of his rage, and I had to acknowledge that my deepest pleasures and resources, including music, had less and less connection to him.

I can hardly remember what there was—two young people who met in an orchestra, duos in the moonlight (like that perfume ad where the violinist sweeps the pianist off her feet), diamond engagement ring, parties, traditional wedding, congratulatory cards containing every cliché ("make sweet music together," "play together, stay together," "musical marriage made in heaven"). We had high hopes, a tiny apartment made artfully cozy, and tons of photos recording the slow, insidious decline, a result of interlocking neuroses and colliding temperaments: his anger and bitterness intimidated me, leading me along the road of passive resistance.

To everyone else, our lives seemed enviable. We took exotic trips, thanks to Rod's business. We gave concerts, although no one ever knew with what tension those were prepared. If he became enraged during a practice session as a result of a difference in interpretation or insufficiently subservient accompaniment, he might hit me on the head with his bow or threaten to destroy my piano. But to the outside world we were loving music-makers constantly being told what an ideal couple we were. In fact, I was downright afraid of him and had no clue how to extricate myself from our mismarriage.

As Rod slept, I propped up my painting. How different it was from the colorful little hand-painted murals all over the walls of our bungalow. I mused about the painters, whoever they were; their naive depictions were cheery and decorative. Would they have understood my loose, impressionistic style?

The toothless old watchman hesitatingly approached me on the little patio, hands mysteriously behind his back. He had seemed fearsome the day of our arrival; indeed there had been rumors of his connection to the Tonton Macoute, the armed underground secret service henchmen of Jean-Claude Duvalier's regime. He gently brought forth two exquisite conch shells, grinning sheepishly. Flustered, I explained that my purse was inside and my husband was asleep. Then with a flush I realized my gaucherie: despair flitted across his face, and he insisted, in Creole, "Mais non, madame. C'est un cadeau!" I thanked him for his gift and went inside.

The unpaved road sent up clouds of dry dust, yielding two grim options—sweltering inside a closed car or becoming coated with grime. I tied a cotton scarf around my hair and put my sunglasses on. I could feel the perspiration and dust cake into muddiness and Rod's irritability mount.

"Who the hell is he anyhow? If you want to get involved with strange men you meet on beaches, go on your own vacation."

"Rod, please don't start again. His offer came out of sincere hospitality. It's a privilege to be invited to someone's home, and not just be confined to hotel culture. Isn't it better to go around with someone who knows a place?"

"Maybe for you. When I go on vacation, it's to get away from people. But you have to get us trapped into luncheons and tours."

The small Fiat had become a veritable oven. I focused on the scene: all along the road were beautiful women, some in their market dresses, others in rags, carrying ungainly loads of produce on their heads. I was deeply moved that although they were doing the work of beasts of burden, their body language and carriage bespoke the same dignity and self-esteem as the higher-class women on the beach. The little girls had big satin party bows in their hair; tiny sway-backed shacks, propped up on toothpicks, were gaily painted; even the donkeys wore ornaments. A spirit of vitality and optimism prevailed in spite of the poverty and hardship. A couple at the hotel told me that their car had broken down on a remote part of the island. They lay down on the grass to rest while waiting for it to be repaired, and when they awoke, there were fresh linens under their heads! Everywhere the Haitian people's generosity and good cheer were palpable.

We parked and I spotted Sergo standing with his hands in his pockets observing the antlike activity in the streets. He saw us and walked over.

"*Bonjour.* Some crowds, eh? Today is market day. Would you like to see it?"

We walked two blocks to the Iron Market. Buses painted bright as carousels, with names like *Bonheur, L'Esperance,* and *Jolie Madame,* rattled by. In the streets the *élites* brushed shoulders with armless beggars.

I could bear it only as a kaleidoscopic composite of brilliant fragments, through squinted eyes. The moment I focused on a single human face, I felt pain. Swarms of people swirled in and out of narrow alleyways between fragile matchbox structures. A beggar whose kindly visage neutralized his grotesque disfigurement turned his face discreetly as he offered his hat, his instinctive gentility and grace transcending his demoralizing condition.

Inside the enormous iron structure, formerly a railroad station, the din was punctuated with the shrieks of vendors, and we were accosted from all sides. Sergo's firm "Pas aujourd'hui" (Not today) seemed to clear a path. Wood carvings, primitive paintings, fruit, fish, poultry, live cattle, embroidery, weavings, shells, baskets, mats, beads, tortoiseshell, amber—in each stall, vendors taut with hope.

"If you buy anything, you will be instantly surrounded by a thousand others. Wait and we will go into a shop if you want to buy."

The street seemed a refuge by comparison to the stifling heat, melange of smells, and turbulence inside. Sergo took us to an art gallery on the second floor of a handsome wooden colonial building. The gallery owner was Parisian and treated him with great respect. "I heard you were back. We must have a drink and talk soon."

Back in the street, Rod went to purchase film while Sergo gave me directions to his home in Pétionville, a suburb in the hills above Port-au-Prince, where his mother expected us in twenty minutes.

Rod pulled our car up to a bank with a grimly set jaw, a dangerous sign of resentment that I knew all too well. He muttered, "Got to cash some checks."

"Please don't lose sight of the time. They expect us very soon."

I waited in the unbearably hot car. There was classical music being broadcast loudly from the bank, and a classical music station on the radio. I had plenty of time to reflect on the incongruity of the music in that setting and the irony that music was so curiously incidental in my relationship with Rod. We could barely practice together anymore because of our different temperaments and tastes—differences that permeated all the rest of our existence as well. He was slow and methodical, compulsive about details, chronically late. I was quick, spontaneous, impatient with his over-scrupulous ways, always on time. I was casual, social, upbeat, and generally happy; he was what my mother had termed a "heavy" as far back as the week of our marriage. Responsible? Yes. Reliable? Yes. Serious? Yes. Joyful? Never.

Perhaps the fact that I came from an economically insecure house made the prospect of life with a serious, reliable young man seem like paradise to me. And for some years we did coast on the waves created by the mythical union of violin and piano. But the slow encroachment of what I began to think of as illness began to awaken me from my lethargic state of unreality. It had gone on too long unacknowledged, denied under the catchall term "stress." I had gotten into a reckless acceptance that this was what life had to offer. Rod always rationalized, "Real life isn't like the movies," and I bought into it, counting my blessings, and concluding, *Well, I just don't have a good marriage.*

We were already late. I went into the bank to look for him. He had finished his transactions and was meticulously folding bills into his wallet. I said carefully, "Do you know what time it is?" He did not respond, only glowered. I left, and he followed me to the car, his cheek flexing as he gritted his teeth in anger. Slamming the door, he stamped the gas pedal down to the floor, backing the car out with a violent jolt. I started to tremble.

He snarled, "Do you realize how you embarrassed me in the bank?"

"How did I do that?" I asked, modulating my voice with great caution to mask my fear, as one does to a mad dog.

"You shouted across a million people to rush me."

"I asked you quietly if you were aware of the time, and walked out."

"You shouted."

I recognized the danger signs and decided not to respond, to try to defuse his behavior.

"Admit you shouted, you filthy bitch! That's the last time you'll ever do that. You'll be lying dead in the gutter before you open a mouth like that."

With one sudden swipe he struck me on the side of the head at arm's length across the front seat. I thought, as I had thought before on the 59th Street Bridge in New York City, the London Tollway, the German Autobahn, *I will open this door and fall onto the road and it will be a quick end. Don't cry. You'll give him satisfaction and you'll look lousy. Don't cry, he's not worth it. . . . Do cry. Cry for your life. Your lost life with this creep.* I cried. Besides, my crying always seemed to assuage his temper. And then I looked out the window and saw the enormously high red poinsettias and the wonderful stone walls along the winding road. Over the wall were the dry hills and goats and distant shacks, all in the same *coup d'oeil* with the beautiful gingerbread colonial homes of Pétionville. I thought, *Thank you, God, that even when I want to die, I can still see the beauty and want to live.*

We arrived at rue Verdon and were greeted by Sergo, his mother, and their dog. I smiled, and Rod smiled. Sergo's brow was furrowed with concern. From his quizzical glance I realized, *I've known this man one day, and he has more understanding for what I feel than the man I have been married to for ten years.*

Sergo's family and servants had prepared a banquet, and we were fêted with a hospitality and kindliness that personified the whole Villefranche residence. It was a memorable feast: plantain pancakes, wild rice with native black mushrooms, langouste, papaya, and a mocha mousse with rum. By the time the strong Haitian coffee was served, I felt queasy. I made a supreme effort to conceal my increasing discomfort, but with instinctive maternal concern, Madame Villefranche came in with a linen cloth saturated with iced rum. She gently applied the compress to my forehead, murmuring "Pauvre petite!" as she ministered to me. The effects were instantly curative and soothing. I was transported by angels' wings back to my own childhood, my own mother giving me an alcohol rubdown when I was ill, and I experienced a wave of love for the universal institution of motherhood. In the four days left to our vacation, Sergo came twice more to the hotel. He escorted us to a nearby fishing village, delicately suggesting that we follow him in our car. I sat silently beside my husband, longing to be in the other car. Sergo's calm spirit was contagious, and I felt that he was acting no longer as tour guide, but rather as protector.

He appeared at the airport for our departure with a gift from his mother.

"You must wait to open it on the plane." Those were the only words he uttered, and I did not allow myself to look at him for fear of crying. I counted the number of people in front of me before I would have to pass through the gate that would finally separate me from the unexpected realm of sweetness I had found.

Rod presented the tickets, and now I had to proceed. With great physical effort I forced my eyes to Sergo's and we exchanged a look of piercing understanding and deep friendship. His eyes seemed to tell me, *You will be all right. You are strong, worthy, and lovable.* All I could hope was that on my face he could read, *Thank you.* Tears were welling up and I turned quickly to the plane.

From my seat I watched my new friend in his crisp white shirt, both arms waving, until I could see him no more. The plane gained altitude and soon the enormous mountains and valleys blurred together into one hazy mass. I was overwhelmed by a sense of small islands and huge oceans.

I truly thought I would never see Sergo again, and I made an honest effort to forget him. But whenever pain and chaos threatened to overtake me, his image superimposed itself and calmed me down. I had started a diary after returning home, and slowly that diary metamorphosed into a correspondence with him, in French. I rented a postal box for privacy and safety. His letters were missives of support and encouragement. I sent him tapes of my concerts, and he began to urge me to expand my arena of expectation, suggesting all manner of concerts and tours, which I had only dreamed of before then. Then one day he wrote that he was coming to the United States, and I was engulfed in panic. There was no question but that he could not stay with us. Rod had no idea of our correspondence, in fact, rarely had the trip to Haiti come up in our conversation during the year since we were there. Sergo made it easy by arranging a hotel in New York, with no presumptions on our hospitality.

On two separate occasions while he was in New York City, I took the train to spend a day with him. In Haiti, my only thought of skin color was that I had felt anemic and pale beside the brown-skinned population; in New York, I was somewhat discomfited by the attention we got sitting in a restaurant, walking in the street, browsing in shops. It was the first time since the day I had met him on the beach that the notion of race or ethnicity had ever entered my thoughts, and now there were moments I had to concentrate hard to fend off my awareness of our different backgrounds. But the calming effect he had on my whole being still prevailed.

"Sergo, I never played for you live. I have a crazy idea. Let's go to a piano store and make believe that we want to purchase an instrument." So we walked to the area around Seventh Avenue where piano stores abound and entered a shop.

I already felt myself in a state of daring and intrigue just from having met him in the city without telling a soul where I was going; I was exhilarated by the feeling that I was living a fantasy, and so I stepped outside of myself and said to the salesman, "My friend is the governor of an island country in the Caribbean. How difficult would it be to transport a piano to his residence, and what are the recommendations for the care of pianos in that region?"

The salesperson responded with no sign of surprise at my questions. "Madame, we send pianos all over the world with no problems at all."

"May I play a few of your instruments so he can get a sense of the size and resonance?"

"Certainly. Make yourselves at home. I will leave you alone, and if you have any questions, I'll be right there in my office."

With carte blanche to play whatever and however long I wished, I went to the spot at which I was most comfortable in the world, the piano bench, and began to play, while Sergo seated himself on a sofa in the showroom. Chopin nocturnes, Bach preludes and fugues, Schumann pieces, snippets and movements from a strange assortment of repertoire, all reflective of my dissociative and chaotic frame of mind, came forth from the various pianos in the salon. After an hour I thanked the salesman, requested his card, and said we would be in touch.

We walked for several blocks without a word, and then Sergo said, "You have something so special in your playing. Why do you wait so long to play in New York?"

That question was the catalyst for my next action, one I'd been on the brink of for years. I went with Sergo directly to a management agency whose card I had carried around in my wallet for information on renting a recital hall, and thus the gears were set in motion for the realization of my lifelong dream: a debut recital at Carnegie Recital Hall.

On the way home on the train, I remarked to myself how comfortable my friendship with Sergo was, and how interesting it was that the subject or suggestion of sex had never entered our conversation for all those hours together, at the same time as I acknowledged my heightened awareness of myself and all the world around me. Rod would never believe the facts of my day. He must never know, must never be able to take it all away from me.

The moment Sergo returned to Haiti, I set to the task of arranging the details of my New York recital. My inquiries revealed that the hall was booked solid until the following season. I made a down payment on the recital hall, and the moment that was done, my heart began to pound with the magnitude of my decision. I would have ten months to prepare, and I welcomed the opportunity to obviate all else but the monkish devotion it would take to be ready.

But I had to tell Rod, and I dreaded his response. He was always more generous monetarily than emotionally. It wasn't the payment, it was the implication that I was following through without him on a dream that he felt was half his. The reality was that we were poorly paired both in repertoire and temperamentally. The biggest impediment was the tension that always manifested itself in anything we undertook together. As I anticipated, the events that ensued the evening I chose to bring the subject up made the thought of working with any repose at home out of the question. Both my beloved piano and myself had been threatened, and all night I lay awake trying to figure out how to leave him. All through the dark hours beside him (had I left his bed he would have continued to rage), I made intricate plans for the day ahead.

The next day, as soon as I heard his tires crunch over the gravel driveway, I called a moving company to get estimates on moving pianos overseas. I made a list of the bare-essential material possessions without which I could not live: paintings, family albums, some books, clothing, typewriter, paints, a few pieces of pottery, odd objects. As I walked around my lovely home, I realized how I might love any other space better if it contained peace. I knew that with some support from friends and good hard work, I might have a chance at a life dependent only on myself and my own resources.

Sergo had once told me he could provide a refuge for me, a place to work and to think. I knew I could not offer more of myself than my friendship and gratitude, and that he would still welcome me.

I phoned him and he reiterated, "You never have to owe me anything. My mother and I have a huge house here. You will have your own wing. No one will disturb you. The servants will cook for you. You needn't worry about my expectations from you. I have none."

I did believe that he offered me the only alternative for my life at that moment, and I thought of the plan as an interim stage in my life. Sergo would be a true friend and enabler, and Haiti was in a period of relative peace; everything seemed to fit together like a puzzle. Sergo seemed heaven-sent to provide an exit that had eluded me for years.

I probably could have effected the move in one day. My piano and things could have been emptied from the house in the short space of time between the sweet sound of Rod's car rolling out of the driveway in the morning and the fearsome hour of his return. I sat shivering with the weight of such a decision, the image of his terrorizing rage, his searches and queries. I pictured a posse coming after me, even though I knew it would never occur to him that I had fled to Haiti. Maybe it would have been the safest place in the world, in all its unlikeliness. I crafted a cliché of a note in my head—"It's over, don't try to find me. I will have a lawyer phone you."

I owed him absolutely nothing, and I owed myself freedom and peace. As incongruous a thought as it might seem to anyone else in the world, Haiti might be the only place I could find relief; but as I snapped back to reality I knew it would take more than a miracle to get me and my piano there intact: images of the instrument in a truck, bouncing over dusty, pitted roads, of the piano strings rusting from the moist island climate, and of the cultural isolation, above all, subverted my resolve.

I don't know how long I stared into the woods. Eventually I went inside to the piano, determined to throw myself into my work with more passion and energy than ever, and to figure out my future some other time.

Polly and the Piano

AT a time in my life when I had only myself, my projects, and my plans, but no more marriage and just a few close friends, I did have a great dog named Polly. Many a day when my mood was dark and threatening, like the crow who shook the snow off its feathers and onto Robert Frost's head, Polly lifted me up and out into the light again.

At first I had two dogs, one left over from our family days and a pup I got at the pound. Watching them play was one of my most restful and joyous pastimes—their nip-and-tuck tactics, hide and seek, growling their mock anger mixed with glee, racing round and round; they made a playmate out of me simply by my watching them. They cajoled and teased, gave irresistible ear baths to each other, danced interlocked on their hind legs, necks entwined; and when Pookie, the older dog, got tired and angry, Polly, the puppy, assumed the characteristic submissive attitude of her ancestors, lying on her back, but only long enough to appease, and then she was up and at it again in a flash. It always seemed that they were showing off for me. They streaked around the open space of the yard like two black banners, weaving in and out of shrubs, barely grazing them, like slalom racers. A thrown stick or fallen apple added greatly to the excitement. But then, as if by agreement, they would suddenly call it quits. Polly would flop spread-eagled, her four legs going in four directions, after slopping a drink from her water bowl, and Pookie, as if she were the princess with the pea, would collapse on a couch with the fluffiest pillows for a good long nap.

All of our family dogs came from shelters, and all sported the commonest mutt markings—the winsome black and tan variety. Those seemed a prerequisite identification mark for a canine in our household. Polly had a plump muzzle and a substantial head, leading to my loving nickname for her, "Boxhead." Her beautiful amber eyes were made even more expressive by two tan brows that seemed to move sympathetically with each of her thoughts. She had chunky paws that always seemed to smell of popcorn, and unmatched ears, one of which was usually cocked. Her tail was crooked at the end, and she had a white stripe down her belly that stayed downy soft, like angel hair, while all the rest of her fur was wiry.

Of all of our dogs, Polly was the most docile and eager to please. She was the best darn dog I ever had. If I went out to the market and said in a firm voice, "Stay!" she would sit outside patiently on the front doormat until my return. She had a variety of tricks, but she amused me the most when she responded to my commands in French: "Donnes la patte," and she gave her chubby paw; "viens ici," and she came; the word "voiture" sent her pirouetting in circles until I took her for a ride in the car.

When Pookie died, Polly's spirits took a dive, and we were like two zombies for a while. It was around then that I decided to give another New York recital, and I threw myself into the preparation with a monastic sort of regimen. Since the very first day I took Polly home from the shelter, her basket was underneath my piano. It was a strange doghouse, but she always seemed to like the vibrations and big black roof over her head. During the hours I was at the piano, she stayed nearby on a chair or underneath the piano in her basket, and inevitably at a certain moment she came over to the pedals, settling her now chunky body somewhere near my feet (sometimes *on* my foot) so that if I kicked my shoes off, I could have my own private foot-warmer. She never disturbed me when I was deep into my work, but she knew intuitively when I was growing tired, and often nudged me with her furry muzzle to remind me to take a break. In such ways did we become inextricably bound.

Polly greeted all of my students, anticipating each arrival with a tensed posture until she saw them appear at the door, whereupon her tail would begin to wag like a metronome. Each student received Polly's deluxe welcoming routine, and the dog's presence was a bonus part of the lesson experience. When I had group classes or recitals at home, she was never underfoot—she took her place on the large triangular landing halfway up the staircase and watched the proceedings like a critic.

As the New York recital date approached and my nerves worked on my physical state, I did yoga, treated myself to massages, practiced meditation, and conjured up a delightful fantasy that I still, to this day, wonder about. Would it have been so improbable to act out? I started to tell Polly, during my practice sessions, that I was going to take her with me to Carnegie Recital Hall. The thought amused not only me—it apparently amused her: I was talking to her in such a serious new voice that she cocked her head and elevated her ears in an irresistibly cute, attentive way. This little game took the edge off my tension, adding a blithe note to the long hours. I invented little scenarios of us both backstage. The truth is that studies have shown that animals do, indeed, lower blood pressure, slow the rate of heartbeats, and generally improve the health of those who choose to live with them. It seemed to me that it would be great to have her with me backstage, to run my fingers through her woolly fur, instead of wringing my hands. But my fantasy did not end there. I imagined myself walking out onto the stage, with Polly on a leash, and having her settle down, as was her wont, at the pedals, sitting patiently through every selection on the program, then accepting the applause alongside me, which certainly was her due as my main supporter and companion all throughout the preparation.

It was a lovely fantasy, but alas, I had to go it alone. I seem to be able to do these formidable feats called solo recitals and land on my feet, but the toll exacted beforehand is considerable; I always swear, just about a week before the concert, that this will be the last time. Would anybody really mind if Polly were there with me? Yes, I would be considered extremely eccentric, but that could be my gimmick! Somewhere there is a topless cellist; I could be the pianist with the dog.

A couple of years after that recital, I met an almost-perfect man who was to become the love of my life. His main flaw was that he was not a dog person. If I had been forced to choose between him and my dog when we decided to live together, I'm sorry to go on record here as saying I would have continued to live alone with Polly and have my love go home to sleep in his own house! Thankfully it never came to that. Ernest wanted to be with me and decided that he would make certain accommodations.

Until the day he moved in, Polly slept upstairs in the bedroom with me, on a mat on the floor. Ernest begged me to compromise and have the dog stay downstairs. I was willing to try, but I had my doubts whether a five-year-old dog could learn this new habit. On the eventful day that Ernest moved in, the first time that Polly put a paw on a step to go upstairs, as she had done for all the years of her life, I held her firmly at the collar and said, in the deepest, sternest voice I could bear to use on my exemplary dog, "No." She looked at me to check out my intentions—had she actually heard that scolding tone from me when she knew she had done nothing to deserve it? And when she ascertained that she had, indeed, received the command to desist from mounting the stairs, she stopped in her tracks and never put a paw there again (until we changed the rules). She was the best darn dog there ever was.

The three of us lived well together for a good number of years. We elevated Polly a few notches to a level halfway up the stairs where I placed a mat on the broad landing, and Ern learned to love her. When she was about fourteen and very ill, he and I grieved together. An itinerant veterinarian came to minister to her at home in those last few months, since she was too ill to jump into the car and trembled in anticipation of a medical appointment. Most of the time she lay in her basket under the piano, and we often stretched out on the carpet alongside, visiting with her. My students crouched down to pay their respects, and she seemed to be contented with her passive participation in my musical life.

On a certain designated day, the vet came to take Polly out of her misery. My son and his wife were visiting, and the four of us knelt around her basket under the piano, stroking her, whispering sweet talk, and popping an occasional chocolate kiss into her mouth, much to the dog's disbelief. A fifth person, the vet, crawled under the big black instrument with a tranquilizing needle and found a space between our caressing hands to inject it into her thigh. In moments, Polly was sleeping deeply, and then the second, lethal, needle followed. I bent down to kiss her goodbye, and Ern and I left the room in tears as my son and his wife carried her in the basket out to the car.

Polly's ashes are scattered in the woods way in the back, but her sweet spirit is right under the piano, a warm presence as I work.

Paris

I WAS in Paris at least a half a dozen times with the wrong person. My first trip there with Ernest canceled out all the times that I had suffered the pangs of chronic estrangement and hostility in a city made for lovers.

My Paris days began when I was a young mother and won a trip to Europe as one of many prizes on a television quiz show. That triggered a kind of wanderlust, resulting in my ex-husband's determination to work in the airline industry. It could have been an adventuresome existence for us both; instead we brought our tensions to the streets of England, France, Italy, Denmark, and Switzerland, through the Far East and into the South Pacific. But I met some very interesting people, each one a tale worth telling, and for that I am grateful.

One day while I was on line in the cafeteria of the Museum of Modern Art in New York, I asked a distinguished-looking older man standing behind me whether he would hold my spot while I made a phone call. When I returned, I thanked him, and he, in turn, asked me to hold his spot for him. Afterward, we began to talk about the current Cézanne exhibit, and he politely asked me if I would mind if he sat at the same table. (This practice was common until the newer, expanded café was installed.)

"Certainly not," I replied, and for the next half-hour we shared some lively conversation ranging the world of art and music, until he rose and offered his card to me: M. Emil Merton, avenue Foch, Paris, France.

"If you and your family are ever in Paris and I can be of service to you, please let me know." He bowed courteously and was off, leaving me musing about what it is I love about New York, museums, art, and life.

Some months later, in fact, my children and I would be accompanying my husband on a business trip to Paris. The Monet gardens at Giverny were just being restored and were not yet open to the public. It occurred to me that perhaps Monsieur Merton, with his connections in the art world, might be able to facilitate a visit to Giverny. So I wrote him: "I wonder if you recall a brief conversation we had at MOMA in New York about six months ago, at which time you were kind enough to give me your card. . . ."

By return mail I received his note: "I do, indeed, remember our conversation. I would be most happy to try and see what the situation is with Giverny, but meanwhile my wife and I would love to have you and your family join us for dinner at home and share our modest collection of paintings. Please be sure and phone us as soon as you arrive and we'll make further plans."

I recognized the rarity of an invitation into a private French home but, alas, it was just another memorable opportunity in my life that had to be left unrealized. When I enthusiastically related the episode to my husband, including the unusual invitation, his response stunned me: "I'm not interested in meeting any of your pick-ups. Go yourself, if you want to."

Of course I could not. Smitten with pain, anger, and embarrassment for the way this experience would be aborted, I wrote a note to M. Merton "explaining" that my husband had scheduled business dinners and appointments for us every evening and we would, very regrettably, have to decline his kind invitation." (My ability to invent excuses over the years was developed by my husband's antisocial tendencies.)

I recounted the Paris-related episode to Ernest a few weeks before our departure. "But you must write him now!" he insisted.

"Ernie, he may be dead for all I know! It's been twelve years, he was already elderly, and I only spoke to him for a short time. Even if he is still there, he'll never remember me."

"Honey, if he's alive, he'll remember you and the lively conversation. Judging from his letter to you, it made a lasting impression on him as well."

I wavered. "He'll think I'm a crazy woman looking for a second invitation. He'll never understand why I took so long to write back."

Ernie replied, "You'll find a way to write him discreetly, and your experience will pick up exactly where it left off. Write!"

So I wrote:

This may be the strangest letter you will ever receive as it almost negates the passage of twelve years' time. I am enclosing a letter you wrote me then, in which you so kindly extended an invitation to my family for a visit that never materialized.

To put it briefly, that trip was the beginning of the end of my marriage, and many things fell by the wayside. Now I am very happily remarried to a man who shares my enthusiasm for art *and* life and we are coming to Paris in December. I certainly do not expect you and your wife to re-extend any invitations, but if there were a chance we four might meet for an hour for an apéritif and some good conversation, we would love it.

If you think these are the scribblings of a crazy woman, let me just say that your generosity and kindness made a deep impression on me that survived through the years until this return to Paris under a happy star.

As Ernest believed, and I didn't dare to hope, M. Merton's letter arrived in our mailbox ten days later:

Of course I remember you! Didn't I have the cheek to sit at your table at the MOMA cafeteria?

The charming and somewhat miraculous invitation to their home for dinner was what I needed for final reconfirmation of myself.

Our trip got off to a bad start. My friend Betsy had come to drive us to the airport that Friday evening, and just as we were leaving the house, Ernest chanced to glance at the tickets and noticed with shock that they read: departure *Sunday* evening. I went into orbit at the travel agent's error: we were booked into a hotel on Saturday and expected at the Mertons' on Sunday.

As usual, Ernest dealt with the situation with an annoyingly exemplary combination of calm passive acceptance, good nature, and rational thinking, while I angrily phoned the agent's office. She insisted that there was absolutely no way we could, at this late date during a holiday season, get on another flight to Paris, and blamed *us* for waiting so long to check our tickets for errors.

Being the action person I am, sometimes irrational, and in bloody bad humor, with no interest in being exemplary, I was determined we would go that night. Ernie suggested, "We could phone the Mertons and explain the situation, postponing our visit a couple of days. We can pretend we are on vacation at home these two days, not answer the phone, and go out for Peking duck, your favorite."

Inconsolable, I composed a two-word rhyme using the word "duck" and insisted we leave for the airport. So the three of us, two eye-rollers and I, left the house for Kennedy Airport. Betsy double-parked while I ran to the ticket counter and explained the error to the Air France agent. She hastened to inform me that a flight had been canceled, all remaining flights were overbooked, and there was no way she could get us onto a flight this weekend.

Anyone else would have accepted the reality and gone home, but apparently, not me.

"Is the manager here?" I asked.

"No, he'll be here in half an hour."

Ernie and Betsy remained hostages of my stubbornness, waiting in the car while I accosted the next dozen official-looking men who approached the counter until the Air France manager finally arrived. Then I heard myself saying: "Monsieur, you are probably the only man on earth that can help me. My husband and I were meant to leave this evening for Paris, and a mistake was made by the booking agent when we were ticketed. Here is our hotel reservation in Paris for Saturday and here is my press pass—I am supposed to review a concert in Paris tomorrow, or I will lose my job."

While I was speaking the manager was shaking his head hopelessly from side to side, poking his finger around on his computer keyboard and scrutinizing the screen intently. Suddenly his head stopped shaking. He poked a few more keys, looked at me directly, and said, "I will put you on the midnight flight in business class. Here are two passes to the restaurant in the Air France lounge so you and your husband can have dinner while you wait."

I didn't know whether to cry or to prostrate myself at his feet. I kept my composure, thanked him to high heaven, and ran out to the car brandishing my hard-won tickets to my astonished and admiring husband and friend. Somehow I was not so much astonished as relieved; I knew I was meant to go to Paris that night, and I had felt certain I would find the way.

When we arrived at Orly airport, though, my valise was missing. Ernest and I had identical bags, except for the green ribbon I had tied around my handle. We spent the next hour filling out forms, estimating the weight in grams of the missing bag, describing its contents, and leaving behind the address of our hotel in case it was found.

Ernest sympathized, "It's too bad that it wasn't my bag that was lost instead of yours. I could make do with what I've got on until they find it, and I didn't pack such finery as you did." My valise also contained my watercolors and sketchpads, without which I never travel.

Upon arrival at the hotel, we quickly deposited our remaining luggage and hurried out to Au Printemps department store to purchase a few necessities for me such as lingerie and some toiletries. Even more unpleasant than the thought of losing the choice articles of clothing that I had purchased for this trip was the experience of being scanned from head to toe by elegant, *soignée* salesgirls trying to determine my size in French. In fact, I soon concluded that the only negative aspect of a visit to Paris is one's constant self-assessment in comparison with the average Parisian woman. (This is not true for the rest of France.)

When we returned with our few overpriced, undersized garments, the concierge informed us that our missing valise had been found and delivered. We hurried up to our room in the tiny *ascenseur* and quickly unlatched the bag, only to find Ernie's shirts and underwear folded squarely on top. We had inadvertently packed in each other's luggage. We sat ourselves down on the floor and gave way to maniacal laughter, releasing the tension that had been mounting from the moment Ernest had discovered the error in our booking.

We could finally take stock of our quite French room and tiny balcony outside two large windows ornamented with iron grillework, the little *cabinet de bain,* the flocked floral wallpaper, a chenille bedspread, and to cap it all off, a view of Boulevard Raspail in Montparnasse, where every restaurant seems to have memorabilia from its fabled artists' population: La Coupole, Le Dôme, La Rotunde.

On our first walk after a brief nap, we happened upon the *atelier-cum-petite-musée* Zadkine. Ernest knew the work of this great Russian-born sculptor and good friend of the painter Modigliani from his art history student days. This was the first of many discoveries in the neighborhood around our hotel. We bought goodies from the corner *boulangerie,* visited the illustrious *cimetiaire,* and studied the bus network and schedules. Our first Parisian dinner was in an excellent seafood establishment where they piled the layers of *crevettes* (shrimp), *huîtres* (oysters), *langouste* (lobster), and other less identifiable sea creatures in mounds on a multitiered serving tray. It seemed that all of Paris and their dogs were sitting there at (or, in the dogs' cases, under,) the tables. Except for the cigarette smoke in all restaurants and dog droppings on the sidewalks, being in Paris was a dream.

It was an easy bus ride to the Arc de Triomphe, from which we walked along the elegant avenue Foch to the Mertons' building. I remembered that this had also been the address of Arthur Rubinstein and his family. The grand boulevard with its *belle époque* buildings seemed incomplete without the horse-drawn carriages depicted in great impressionist paintings. It was in fact like walking through an artwork. It was snowing lightly, and the dusting of white enhanced the magical wedding-cake appearance of the ornate facades.

We walked through a courtyard into an outer lobby with a directory of names and rang a buzzer, through which a kindly voice commanded "Entrez!" And there in the rather imposing inner sanctum was the elderly, somewhat shrunken Monsieur Merton, whose kindly visage was only remotely familiar from that scant half-hour of conversation so many years ago. (But that's the wonderful thing about New York: the comfortable ease with which people can engage in a light exchange and end up in a magnificent Parisian setting twelve years later.) The three of us just made it crammed into the tiny *ascenseur,* alighting on a floor that seemed to be his entire domain.

Madame Merton entered the room, clearly a delicate gentlewoman of high taste and culture. She greeted us in English, her pretty face illuminated by a warm and welcoming smile. She had fine white hair drawn up in a chignon and a paisley shawl around her shoulders. For the rest of our visit, life seemed to imitate art: a continuous succession of settings from paintings, mostly salons and interiors from Vuillard; carpets, tapestries, patterns upon patterns, relieved by pale-ochre walls upon which hung paintings clearly recognizable as works by Soutine, Utrillo, Sisley, Denis, Ernst, Chagall, and many more. I tried to walk the narrow line between being openly awestruck and simply displaying the sheer bliss of experiencing these works in a home setting. Viewing artwork in an intimate salon environment, rather than in a museum, is akin to the extraordinary experience of making music in a true *chambre de musique* just as Chopin preferred to do. I reverently eyed the Mertons' lovely old Pleyel piano from the 1880s, covered with marquetry and carving.

"Will you play?" Monsieur asked gently.

I responded with the *Barcarolle,* my favorite Chopin work, which the composer truly believed was composed for a smaller space than a concert hall. I couldn't stop myself; the thin yet pearly character of the instrument was so true to the sound for which this music was conceived. I followed with a string of mazurkas, waltzes, and a ballade. My fantasy was that Chopin himself might have played this very piano had he lived that long, and I couldn't have asked for three more rapt listeners. It was a fair swap: the music in return for the art. Then came a light but delicious supper with aged Bordeaux wine, *boeuf bourgignon,* and a green salad. *Tarte aux fraises* from their local boulangerie and *café filtre* ended the memorable meal.

The conversation was too rapid, charged, and scintillating to reconstruct. The miracle was that we had not known this couple before, we probably would never see them again, yet we connected with each other on a deep level born of our mutual appreciation of great art. We were intensely affected by their sincere pleasure in sharing the masterworks of which they modestly professed to have only custodial propriety and walked back to the hotel, possibly two miles under gentle snow, high in spirit.

The next day, Christmas Eve, we returned the items we bought at Au Printemps, and Ernie insisted on buying me a beautiful black velvet couturier opera coat, which has become my official concert wrap. It is the single most beautiful piece of clothing I own. We browsed the *bouquinistes* (bookstalls) along the Seine; I found some old music, most notably a hardcover edition by Maurice Ravel of Felix Mendelssohn's *Songs without Words.* We climbed to the tower of Notre Dame cathedral, after which I thought my heart would give out until I saw a very old woman climbing the endless spiral staircase just behind me grin and exclaim, "C'est formidable, n'est-ce pas?" We stayed for the Christmas Eve mass. The huge dark cathedral was mobbed. Flickering candles dripped all over the place, and while the litanies, prayers and liturgical organ music were reverberating through the mighty vaults, I tried to sketch whatever vignettes I could spy between the shoulders of worshippers on every side.

The best museum of all in Paris is the street, and finally I was walking there, among lovers, with my lover. We went to the Louvre. (This was the Paris of the pre-pyramid Louvre and the under-construction Musée d'Orsay.) The dreary halls of the Louvre were relieved by the comical collections of tourists piled up around the predictable attractions. The most overheard phrase, intoned in Franglais, was "Où est la *Mona Lisa?*" so I sketched the backs of fifty-odd viewers straining to see a fragment of the smirking *La Gioconda.* In the smaller museums, for example, in the Musée Japonais, we found unheard-of treasures: ten or twelve Vuillards, rare as hen's teeth, all in one gallery. We visited Beauborg, that hideous high-tech structure built for modern art that seems to be inside out, with all its pipes and guts exposed. Perhaps the most beautiful museum was the Musée Picasso, a former mansion, which housed Picasso's art collection along with his own works, where I fell in love with Diego Giacometti (the lesser-known brother of the sculptor Alberto), whose chandeliers, tables, and ornaments embellish the mansion. From the *deuxième étage* I sketched the circuitous queue of people waiting to get into the museum, winding from the inner courtyard out onto the street.

One afternoon we went to the illustrious Conservatoire de Paris, where such luminaries as Alfred Cortot still lend their magical spirits to the halls. I interviewed the *directeur* in his stuffy bachelor's apartment for an article in *Clavier.* Outside the school, I noticed, behind an iron grilleworked window, a poster announcing a recital by a woman with exactly the same name as one of my students. Since the concert had already taken place, I squeezed my hand through the rusty bars, gouging my skin in the process, and carefully ripped away the announcement with a minimum of tearing to secure a prized souvenir for my student, who never expected to see "her" name posted outside the Paris Conservatory. (What a truly devoted teacher won't do for a deserving student!)

On New Year's Eve, I put on the one dressy silk outfit I brought, my new velvet coat, and a jaunty pink felt hat that I got in New York but could wear only in Paris, and we walked to Le Dôme, with its festive atmosphere. We were so glad to have made reservations a few days earlier, because every morsel of our very expensive dinner was exquisite, including the tidbits of sea urchin that a couple sitting at the next table offered me right off their own forks after seeing me eye the creature with suspicion. We came back and watched some excellent ballet on television—a tape of Rudolf Nureyev dancing Debussy's *L'après-midi d'un faune.*

There had been Arab terrorist bombings throughout Europe at various airports including Rome and Athens during the course of our stay. A strong military presence greeted us at the airport in Paris on our return trip, and when I passed through the security gates, a loud alarm went off. To my horror and Ernest's, I was detained, frisked, and questioned: "What do you have in that bag?" It was emptied and the answer came up: watercolors in tubes containing chromium oxide, titanium, cadmium and who knows what other hitherto innocuous ores that somehow together triggered a major scene.

I still hold the view that being in exotic places is wonderful, it's just getting there and back that I hate. Even with the right person.

Mazurka in the Bronx

THE halls were lined with seats in which the elderly watched the parade of weekend visitors. Tiny, shrunken, balding, shapeless, lonely people, to whom Ernest and I nodded and smiled along the corridor to the elevator.

"Those two look as though they don't have a care in the world," one said.

"Maybe they know where my shoes are," the other answered.

Not even the colorful posters that hung everywhere could relieve the oppressive sense of fate and the smell of death.

Earlier in the lounge, as I was waiting for visiting hours to begin, my compliment to an overly made-up old lady triggered a monologue: "Oh, thank you! It's just an old hat. My name is Rosie, and I was a hat model in the grandest department store in Vienna. Here's a picture of me sixty years ago before the Nazis came. Wasn't I beautiful? Look how tall I was. Here all my jewels were stolen. You can't keep anything in this place. I think I know who took it, too. My Dutch boyfriend died and left me a lot of money, but my lawyer was a crook. I wouldn't be here now if he didn't rob me. Are you leaving so soon?"

I conceived a response to Rosie in my head that almost allowed me to forget the stench of urine that was part of the atmosphere from the moment you entered the lobby (though, as nursing homes go, this was a good one):

> *You could still model hats, Rosie,*
> *You have that femme du monde chic at 86*
> *And tinges of your cosmopolitan past.*
> *Your rougey cheeks*
> *And almost-deftly-drawn eyeliner*
> *Could still attract some dapper codger;*
> *They attracted me.*
> *I believe you, Rosie—*
> *Your aristocratic Dutch boyfriend loved you till he died,*
> *Your lawyer was a crook;*
> *I hope you get the money soon,*
> *Lovely lady from "Vienna, City of my Dreams."*

Actually, the first floor wasn't so bad. It had the lounge and the lobby with its influx of people. We were headed for the fourth floor.

"I'm sorry we didn't bring her a plant. It would give her something to tend."

"Carol, my mother is beyond caring about or for things. Those flowers from the garden are colorful, and we're lucky if she notices them."

Poor Ernie. He would never reconcile himself to having his mother in this place, even though he does not believe in guilt and is the most rational man I know.

We entered Mama's room and found her sitting half-nude on the edge of the bed, getting ready to go to bed, even though it was the middle of the day.

"Ernie, you wait outside. I'll help her dress."

Putting squeamishness aside, I helped my gentle ninety-year-old mother-in-law to get back into her clothes. I was surprised by the turn of my thoughts. *She's not half as bad-looking as I thought a ninety-year-old woman would be—pearly, silky soft, translucent skin, glorious white hair, pendulous but touchingly sweet breasts. With some luck I won't look worse at that age and Ern will still be with me, both of us with all our marbles.*

Someone had coiffed her hair, put rouge on her cheeks, and brought her back some of her feminine vanity, possibly in expectation of our weekly visit. She looked kind of elegant, and she was beaming. She had quickly adapted her hostess persona, beckoning us to the folding chairs beside her bed.

I acquired this lovely old gentlewoman along with my second marriage and quickly had to learn some Yiddish since, by the time I met her, she was lapsing back into her childhood amalgam of Yiddish and Polish. I picked some of it up from Ernie, as he sometimes spoke playfully to Polly, our dog, in Yiddish. I amused myself and Ern by springing a new phrase on him and his mother. In her more alert moments, she, too, got the humor of the incongruity of those words coming from me. But in the four years I'd known Ernest, I had witnessed the decline of Mama's life and spirit. By now the fragile thread to which she clung threatened to snap at any moment. There wasn't much humor or amusement left in her life.

Ernie went up to the fifth floor to get a wheelchair, and when he returned he was visibly amused.

"What happened up there, that you're so busy chortling to yourself?"

"Four old ladies sitting all in a row looked me over and one asked, 'Do you have the time, sonny boy?' You see, Carol, it's all a question of relativity, as Einstein said!"

We wheeled Mama out into the garden, a welcome relief from the visits to the drab canteen for tea all winter. As she rolled through the halls, Mama pointed to Ernie and proudly announced to everyone we passed, "Mein sohn!" She had regressed to addressing him by his childhood nickname, Srulik, even though his curly, once-golden locks were gray. When she called me "Carol," it was like some kind of thrilling recompense. We found a sunny spot protected from the wind. An old man walking too briskly to be a resident there went ten times around the circular path.

When he passed again, I asked him, "Are you preparing for the Olympics?"

Grateful for conversation, the man came over and replied in a heavy European accent, "This is nothing! I do this twice every day. I'm only seventy-seven but you know why I stay here? The beautiful women! No, kidding aside, my wife upped and left me five years ago. Dropped dead on me. So I ask you, what was left? I was afraid by me. Put three locks on my doors and shut myself in at five every day. Never opened the windows. What for I should stay there? Here they cook for me—I wouldn't boast about the cooking, but it's three meals a day. I'm getting so fat. It's not bad. At least I'm not scared anymore. Hey mister, you got good taste! The wife is cute!"

"That's my son and his wife," Mama ventured.

The man continued on his constitutional.

"That's not a bad compliment he gave me," I giggled. We turned our attention back to Mama, and Ernie said, "Mama, look how lovely the trees are! It's springtime. Do you see the birds?"

I thought, *He is beautiful and tender with her, but it's like a child's primer: "See the birds. See them fly." Does she find him too indulgent? Patronizing? Or is she truly a child again? Is it a full circle?*

Aloud: "Mama, do you like my crazy earrings? Listen, they jingle when I shake my head." She actually smiled. It occurred to me, *She was a girl once, and she remembers her lovely things. Or maybe that's my fantasy.*

On the way in again, we passed the empty auditorium where someone was putting up May Day decorations. So often I was struck by the inappropriateness of the "entertainment" there: the belly dancer on Father's Day, and now the notion of any of the residents knowing what to do with a maypole, much less dance around it, was absurd. But my own fleeting quasi-altruistic plan to give a recital there would have been just as silly: snoring, coughing, fidgeting, apathy. Even the ambulatory residents of senior institutions that are brought to library recitals in our town fall asleep or talk during the programs, causing distractions for the serious listeners.

Just the same, I suddenly said to Ernie, "There's a piano in there. Wheel her in and I'll play for her."

"Mama, would you like to hear Carol play a concert just for you?"

Mama barely responded. Her mouth with its new ill-fitting dentures seemed to want to utter, *Do with me what you will.*

"She seems to know what she wants to say but somewhere between knowing and being able to find the right words, there's a short circuit."

"Well give it a try, honey, and see if she likes it."

I opened the lid of the grand piano, not a bad instrument—a used Steinway, probably donated by someone—and sat down to play some Chopin mazurkas that Mama had actually danced to in her living room just two years earlier. When she was a young girl in Poland, dancing was one of her greatest pleasures, one she passed along to her son, much to my delight.

Ernie exclaimed, "That's the clearest proof of 'music hath charms' that I ever saw! Look at her face!"

Her face was transformed and illuminated into a young woman's. She sat forward, eyes twinkling, smiling, clapping her hands. In another moment she might have risen right out of the wheel chair and danced. She said, "Schone! Zieseh Veibele!" (Beautiful! Sweet wife!) and I thought, *This is the best damn little recital I ever gave.*

Back in Room 407, I looked out the window and prayed. *Please*

56

God, Don't let me ever end up in a place like this. Let me kill myself first. But these old folks don't do themselves in. Could they, even if they wanted to? (Is it possible that when confronted with the alternative, even this is better?) Maybe I could make it here. I'd bring along my watercolors, and paint the tenements out the window, and the sad faces leaning out of the windows, the elevated trains in the distance like little toy train layouts, and the Spanish grocery with all the produce across the street, the one or two trees, the clouds. . . .

I'd go around from room to room—Ha! There I am! The only ambulatory one, painting the semi-corpses lying on their beds, the heroic nurses, the orderlies, the bitter Filipino doctor who, after years of hard schooling, seemed so disappointed at ending up here on the fourth floor of the Jewish Home and Hospital for the Aged doing only geriatrics when, in fact, his work was valiant. I'd paint them over and over until the portraits reflected the lives behind the faces—the joy and glamour of hat-modeling in Vienna, of folk-dancing in Poland. I probably could survive it if I lost all my sense of smell by then.

Ernie cut into my meditations. "Come, Carol, let's go. She's out like a light. That fresh air was the first she's had after a cooped up winter."

"OK. Put the flowers where she can see them when she wakes up, so she'll remember we were here."

"Don't worry about it."

We were silent a long time in the car as we drove by the billboards, the boarded-up buildings with their *trompe l'oeil* windows painted in, the litter along the parkway. The scene wasn't pretty. I turned to look at Ernie's handsome profile silhouetted against the light of his side window as he drove, noting how similar the features were to his mother's—an older version of him. His pewter-and-bronze hair would eventually turn into her silver. Just as my heart overflowed with tenderness for him, he said to me, "It almost hurts, how much love I feel for you."

The Special Charms of an Old Man

ISEEM to attract old men; the funny thing is that in certain cases I have been curiously attracted to *them*—not sexually, but intellectually, which is a kind of side road into intimacy. I have had some unusual and deeply affecting friendships with quite elderly men, starting with my late, great piano teacher, Leopold Mittman, with whom I studied for over twenty years. His life, his home, his art, and his dedication to me were the greatest influences of my younger life, and we loved each other. Now that Mittman is dead he has become my muse. He left a great void, and that I suppose accounts for the subsequent amities, like the one with Rudolf Harsanyi.

I looked out of Rudi's window facing Central Park while guests assembled for his memorial service. Hawks circled overhead, and I remembered what he had written to me:

> How wonderful that you have kept intact the enthusiasm
> and naiveté of your youth! You drive through Central Park
> in the rain; the blossoming trees are pink and white. You
> look at the still lightly foliaged trees at Central Park West's
> ugly towers and exclaim that New York is as beautiful as
> any city in the world!

It is your joie de vivre that magically transforms New
York into a city as beautiful as Paris, Venice, Florence.
You have the rare gift to poetize the boredom of everyday.
God bless you, my dear.

We first met in the green room after a concert at Avery Fisher
Hall; we were among the throng waiting to greet the pianist, and
Rudi was just in back of me on the line with his dainty Viennese
wife, Agi. She began to quiz me about my background, while
standing on tiptoe, scanning me from head to foot. No one else
could have gotten away with that kind of brazen behavior, but on
her it was curiously beguiling.

Before long Agi, Rudi, and I knew each other's life stories. She
had been the pianist in a trio for many years and now taught
piano privately; he had been with the Associated Press through
the war years and now lectured in art collecting at a small but important art institute. Together they cultivated an illustrious stable
of artistic types, and their home was crammed with relics of a
fascinating past, including sculptures and canvases by their
friends. Antiques were juxtaposed against the most avant-garde
pieces, and it all worked together to form a compelling *gestalt*.
They were an irresistible pair.

Agi was so feisty that she actually once succeeded in having
an airline pilot turn the plane around when she found out that it
was the shuttle headed toward Washington, D.C., and not
Boston, where she had a concert to play that evening. I am certain that she delivered an Academy Award–level performance of
someone having apoplexy so that the poor pilot had no choice.
(This story, of course, predates the current high-security considerations of the airline industry.) She told me that story the first
evening I met her; it was obviously her signature anecdote. Rudi
was still awestruck and enchanted by his wife's unpredictability;

when they were together he usually ceded the floor to her, explaining that he had learned to assume the role of diplomat: a man who thinks twice before saying nothing. The couple were childless, but she knew about love and human nature, and she had intuitions oozing out of every pore. Even in their eighties, they still made love, swam in the nude at their friends' Long Island estate, and were uninhibited about alluding to it.

Rudi enjoyed relating a story about his doctor's suggestion that he swim for his health. In accord with his doctor's orders, he joined the Harmonie Club on Manhattan's Upper East Side, which had a swimming pool that had certain separate days and hours reserved for men and women. "One day, absent-minded as I am, I mixed up the days and walked stark naked into the room with the swimming pool when it was reserved for ladies. Before I realized my faux pas there was screaming and angry shouting. The ladies apparently didn't like what they saw. I turned around, ran back, dressed, left the club, and was later notified by the management that the swimming pool was henceforth out of bounds for me."

Anyone who believes he forgot the right day is more naive than I am.

Agi and I talked about love a lot, and when I met Ernest, whom I wanted for my very own from the start, she hustled her bent-over body to Bergdorf Goodman's and bought me an expensive flacon of Weill's Secret de Venus. With a mischievous wink, she declared, "A few drops in your bath, and he'll be yours forever." I did whatever she told me, and whether that was in any way responsible for my eventual marriage to Ernest, I will never know. But when I told her about our plans to marry, she said triumphantly, "Voilà!"

But unfortunately, she died soon after. Rudi, who loved her well, would have sunk into deeper despair if he hadn't had so many resources. Once, when I commented about his *bon vivant* lifestyle, asking how Agi had ever put up with him, Rudi said, "Agi knew I loved her. She allowed me my little friendships."

"Rudi," I wanted to know, "what is the difference between a 'friendship' and an 'affair'?"

"Oh, that's easy. One is in a bed and one is on a chair."

And that was that. It was the kind of relaxed European attitude I knew I could never embrace, but it worked for them. Rudi played his man-about-town role to the hilt. He took women to lunch and to concerts, and everyone wondered about the man with the magnificent shock of long white hair and strong Hungarian nose coming down the aisle bent over like an L, with two walking canes, just moments before the most important concerts were about to begin.

He was determined to live his life out to the last moment. Rudi didn't only look *distingué,* he was. André Malraux had been his close friend, along with other luminaries—he was especially fascinating on the subject of art and literature. His walls were covered with canvases, sketches, and watercolors, and we spent hours on the subject of good and bad art. He said, "To judge whether a work of art is good, objectively, requires many years of exposure and study. We all make wrong judgments from time to time. Nietzsche wrote that abstaining from wrong judgments would make life impossible." He had the great philosophers' ideas at the ready in his head and could pull them out at the *moment juste.*

He could offer the best explanation for modern abstract expressionism, clarifying for me how those painters discarded everything concrete that might be conjured in the mind of the viewer, even the slightest memory of things seen; he explained that by rejecting representation, intellectual control, and memory, they left only gesture. His own view was that by discarding those elements, abstraction became repetitious and impoverished; he conceded that it took at least several decades for sound judgments, and that art is here to give joy, to enrich life. If it does, it is art; if not, forget about it. It's not exactly my definition, but it's a respectable view. What was so rare about him was that he cared deeply and equally about all the arts.

After Agi died, Rudi moved from their townhouse on the East Side to a small apartment on Central Park West overlooking the park. They had been among the few refugees from the Nazi regime who came away with some wealth from their families. They had often joked about their struggles with Agi's trio, the traveling, the problems in getting booked; but they could afford to joke about it, since they had other resources. Not too many musicians, unless they make it to the top, get to live in the beauty and comfort Agi and Rudi had enjoyed for years. But now he had to pare down considerably to accommodate the smaller space. He took her Steinway piano, most of the wonderful paintings, many of which were portraits of them done by artist-friends, thousands of books that he could read in any one of a dozen languages, and the carpets upon carpets that can transform the plainest domicile into a salon.

The new apartment had a small bedroom, a large living room, and a kitchenette. It was the view that rescued it from being a great comedown from the other address. He placed the piano by the window, and I thought that the vista rivaled any pastoral setting and could inspire hours of good work at the keyboard. Sometimes when I visited, I prepared two gourmet lunches, setting an aesthetically pleasing table for us both for the reward of just listening to him talk. One time, and only once, he introduced flirtation into our friendship with a whopping swat on my backside as I stooped to put out the food. I must say that although it shocked me, I quickly acknowledged to myself that it wasn't a bad swat, that it represented a moment of appreciation for the female anatomy, and that it elevated my own expectations as to how long a person could go on enjoying life in that way.

That afternoon after our luncheon, he read some chapters from the manuscript of my forthcoming book and then, as he invariably did, asked me to play. I never say no when anyone asks me to play, and the combination of his educated ear, the beauty of the instrument, and the view made the experience a great pleasure for me.

When I finished playing he said, "You are the intellectual equivalent of what they call in Hungarian *pâtisseries* a 'three-in-one with whipped cream on top.'"

I always had to take a pile of books off the bench and clear a space for my music. On top of the piano were more piles of books, under the piano even more piles. On every surface of the place there were books. I never saw Rudi unhappier than the time his misguided housekeeper put all his books on his shelves, arranged by size: all the small ones together and so on. He could hardly find any of his beloved treasures and wailed that it would never get straight again; but in a short time, the wonderful chaos he loved to surround himself with was fully restored.

Rudi was the most colorful raconteur I ever met. I never tired of his repertoire of tales dating from his early days as a college student in Vienna. One story left me staggered and haunted for weeks. While he was at the university, he often sat around a particular café that was frequented by the young Jewish intelligentsia. They would engage in philosophical discussions, share essays and poetry, and horse around like any other group of students. One day, probably around 1930, a strange young man entered the café, showed his sketches, and tried to sell them. When there were no takers, he became belligerent, and started making anti-Semitic slurs aimed at the group of students. Soon a brawl broke out, and there was Rudi, inches from this irate troublemaker, and just a tiny impulse away from lifting a chair and cracking it over his head. Had he succumbed to that violent urge, he might have changed the course of history. That angry, hateful young man was Adolf Hitler. This is not an apocryphal tale; that's just the way Rudi's life played out. It was better than any fiction.

Whenever we were all attending the same concert, my husband and I picked Rudi up and took him to the hall or home afterward, to save him the trouble of waiting for cabs. Then we looked forward to lively discussions of the concert spiked with his own quirky observations, such as his dissertation on the violinist Anne-Sophie Mutter's white shoulders. Sometimes an attractive woman would be waiting for him at his seat, a prearranged date; or if he were alone, we would go backstage with him to greet the artist. One evening we spent such a long time in the green room that they had turned off the escalators by the time we were leaving. Rudi would have to climb down two flights of stairs with us, so I suggested, "Rudi, take my arm, and Ernest will walk down the stairs in front of us in case you trip."

"I have a better idea," he said with a straight face. "Let Ernest take my arm. If I fall, I'd rather fall on you."

The one unpleasant episode in our long relationship occurred after a black-tie *soirée musicale* I was presenting in my home. I had broken my leg, and to try to cheer myself up, I gave a dinner party and recital for friends, including my orthopedist and his pretty wife. My ugly white plaster cast was hidden under my long black velvet skirt, and except for the fact that I could not use the *una corda* pedal, the party was going extremely well.

Suddenly I realized that Rudi was making an old fool of himself by pulling the doctor's wife down on his lap, which was more a skeletal bunch of old bones than a real lap. The incident would have been easily discharged as folly, but when he called me the next day to get her telephone number, I felt I had to draw the line. Of course I knew how harmless he was, an eighty-nine-year-old rake, but he was still able, somehow, to ruffle the feathers of my fifty-year-old doctor, and I knew it should stop. Although the doctor's wife could have handled it fine, her husband could not.

I have kept both Rudi's and my letters on this subject, and it is a tribute to both of us that we recovered our friendship after such rancor:

> How come that you are shocked by my decision to break up our relationship after what you have done to me? Must I explain to a woman who, in addition, is a fine, sensitive artist, what it meant for an old man resigned to live out the last years of his life in desperate isolation—and then to fall madly in love in one evening?
>
> You, my friend, had the key to my happiness. All I asked you for was a telephone number. A telephone number. But you struck a holier-than-thou attitude and refused this little service to me, your friend. I wonder what the word friendship means to you? I thought you were my friend. It was an illusion. Good-bye.
>
> P.S. I just got her phone #! So all your self-righteousness was for nothing.

It amazed me that this connoisseur of great literature could not recognize his own scribblings as maudlin melodrama. I wrote back:

> Rudi,
> Then we are both disappointed in each other, because I always admired you for your wit, intellect, and understanding, and your letter had none of these.
>
> As your infatuation (sorry, that is not what I call "love" but we have had that discussion in semantics before) was more meaningful than old friendship, it is *you* who take

friendship lightly. The doctor and his wife are my friends, too, and I made a carefully considered decision based on a very delicate situation.

I certainly do not deserve the kind of childish and punitive letter you write, because I invited you to my home out of real affection and you chose to create a scene which was bound to be troublesome. Be clear that in no way do I begrudge you a moment of romance in your life. But not at the expense of others who happen also to be my friends. What you thought of as playful or intriguing, others found offensive, and a lovely party was turned into a Colette farce. Then, if it's goodbye, then goodbye.

What Rudi didn't know was that the more I thought about it, the more persuasive and pitiable his plea seemed to me, so that in the end, I got a mutual friend to phone him with the telephone number, which in a small way, let me off the moral hook, and which accounted for his adolescent postscript to the letter.

It took him a long time to forgive me, especially considering the limited time we had left. I waited a bit and wrote him a tender letter, and that ended the nonsense. But he certainly took his flirting seriously, even if others did not. He fancied himself one of the world's great *anciens,* ranked with Picasso, Casals, Rubinstein, and Chaplin, with all their bizarre liaisons. He even had a rationale: "Even in heaven they rejoice more at a repenting sinner than at someone who has never sinned." That was funnier to him than it was to me. This fraternity of famous old roués diminished their personas as they went about diminishing the women who fell for them.

Several times I was his chosen companion for lunch, and one afternoon at Sardi's I waited at my table wondering what it would look like to others when my octogenarian date joined me. Wherever he went, heads turned—that Lisztean profile, black fedora, velvet

66

collar, and greatcoat, all evoking the question "Who is he?" A photographer captured him sitting at a chic sidewalk café, and the image appeared in *Gentlemen's Quarterly*. He personified Old World elegance and intrigue.

Rudi chose to start our luncheon date by toasting Agi's *joie*, even though she had been dead two years. I talked about my newfound happiness with Ernest after a twenty-year marriage to a joyless partner. Rudi replied in French, "Les cloches de bonheur sonnent pour tout le monde, mais pas tout le monde l'entendent" (The bells of happiness ring for everyone, but not everyone hears them). Rudi said that for Agi nothing, not even illness, was a trauma. She just could not be unhappy. It was not her nature. We clinked our glasses in celebration of being among the fortunate who hear the bells.

Then Rudi asked me if I would like to have Agi's Steinway piano in my house, to use for my teaching. The question came out of the blue, although he had known how I hated the deterioration of my own piano from all the teaching I did on it. He explained, "I think I would have to store it if you didn't take it, because I haven't enough room for my wheelchair and another bookcase."

I suggested that he allow me to give him some remuneration each month in return for its use. I knew he wasn't exactly giving me the piano; I was sort of keeping it for him, and it would be mutually beneficial. We agreed to a sum that would enable him to take a few women each month to lunch at a good restaurant, and soon the instrument was delivered to my home. Then arrived a treasure trove of music, cartons upon cartons, including original, inscribed manuscripts of chamber music written just for Agi's trio by contemporary composers, hardcover editions of the Beethoven sonatas and *The Well-Tempered Clavier,* and second copies of music I already owned, annotated by Agi and her teachers—a windfall of literature.

For the next year or so I punctiliously sent my "recreation" checks to Rudi, and then one day he put up his hand and said, "Enough. I am glad Agi's piano has a good home." That's how he gave me the most wonderful gift of his beautiful piano. We both agreed about the unique qualities of the instrument, although we differed about Steinways. Rudi preferred the Bösendorfer, which he claimed "sings like a girl in love, while the Steinway sings like a mature, married woman who has a great, secret love affair with a young man." I never asked him how he came up with that analogy.

The three of us went to dinner every now and then, and once when Ernest left the table, Rudi scribbled a note on his calling card and passed it to me: "I love you. Don't tell it to Ernie." It was a joke, of course, which I shared with Ernie as soon as he returned; Rudi was a rogue, and you couldn't take him seriously.

When someone like Rudi writes letters as treasurable as his and tells you that "the enthusiasm emanating from your letters invigorates me," and you love to write anyway, you respond immediately by return mail. I especially loved the relaxed letters he wrote from European spas:

> I come here to pamper the illusion that the baths would
> cure my arthritis. Other illusions are that the world can be
> ruled by goodness and reason, that everybody can be edu-
> cated, that one can understand women, that truth is
> stronger than lies, that one can love one's neighbor, that
> one can understand electrodynamics and relativity; all
> those myths are gone. What remains is only my faith in
> the baths of Bad Ragaz.

He knew it wouldn't really help his old body, but he languished among rich widows and read, read, read. The literature spawned philosophical thoughts, and I was among the lucky recipients of his musings. Not all of them were high-minded:

> I have a nice room with a balcony. A big forest across the street sends cool, aromatic air into my lungs. The service is excellent but the food looks better than it tastes. The guests seem to be uninteresting except a pretty young woman with a charming baby boy (who is a good subject to start a conversation.) With a bit of luck this might become a pleasant vacation.
>
> Give my very best to your greatest admirer. The second greatest admirer sends his love and a kiss and remains your very Hungarian friend anxiously looking forward to your letter.

The availability of attractive women was not the only factor that concerned him. One summer he wrote from Interlaken, Switzerland, about the unwholesome atmosphere of his room: it was very hot and had no air-conditioning. In spite of the breathtaking views and French cuisine, he asked me to pray for a devastating thunderstorm with torrential rains to cool the place down, lamenting, "I wish I'd stayed in good old New York where the air is polluted, the noise unbearable, and where I have to eat the food I cook, but at least in my air-conditioned room."

The next letter from him started: "Getting a letter from you is always inspiring, but you make a big error writing the word *Important!* about enclosing the check. What was important, of course, is the line in which you signed 'Love' to me. How come women don't know what is important in life?"

So many of his missives were filled with the best advice and good humor:

Your long teaching hours are preventing you from using your creative talent fully—which is a pity for creative talent should not be left unexploited.

There are, in my opinion, two ways to liberate you permanently from teaching: the Hungarian and the American way. If you want to take the Hungarian way, you must follow strictly the instructions of "The Hungarian Method of Switching from Labor to Leisure" by the 91-year-old great Hungarian sage and anti-work guru: Immediately after your summer vacation you should promote your better students to assistant teachers. They will teach the rest of your students, which will give you enough free time to write your first bestseller, which will make you rich enough to stop teaching altogether, let Ernie retire, spend the summers in the south of France and the winters, spring, and fall in the Hotel Pierre in New York. You will write more bestsellers, Ernie will walk the dog, you will travel widely, and send me postal cards with your love and best wishes.

The American way consists of buying lottery tickets and waiting for the million. This is easier than writing bestsellers and more likely to get you the million.

I wish you, from the bottom of my heart, many happy, prosperous, and creative years and embrace you very tenderly.

In a long postscript to the same letter, he added:

Your project for this summer "To write, think, and love" is an enviable one, but to deepen your relationship with yourself is more difficult than teaching. Also your chronology is wrong. To "write, think, and love" will not get you very far. You should love, think, and only then, write. Listen to me sweetheart! You are a gifted writer; your prose is clear, fluent, enjoyable; you have had an interesting life. This is a treasure for a writer. Why don't you exploit it and write a book called "Two Marriages: One Bad, One Good."

Thus did Rudi single-handedly go about the business of elevating my self-image. He even sanctioned my spending sprees whenever I was depressed by referring to it as "one of those glorious drives that raptures a woman's heart, especially if it is approved by an uncritical husband."

From Interlaken:

I enjoyed your enthusiastic report on Italy. What a blessing to know a woman of your sensitivity in this callous world full of deceit, snobbism, and pretense! I want to hear more about your trip when I return from Switzerland. I embrace you. Your over-aged Rudi.

Even if he made carbon copies of those sweet words and sent them to each woman he knew, I wager that not a single one wouldn't choose to believe he meant every syllable; such was his persuasive charm. In fact, he *did* mean every word he wrote.

He wrote every fairly attractive woman he ever met. He loved to write to women, and he wrote spectacular letters. I got my goodly share, but one day he showed me a letter and fretted that he couldn't remember to whom he had written it. "But isn't it a beautiful letter?" he lamented.

"Yes, Rudi, it is. So save it, and send it to the next lady you meet and like."

That's how it was with him. If the woman didn't write him

back, that would be it. Or if she did, and she didn't write well, he would say, "She has only her looks and no substance," and lose interest. His most titillating intrigue was when he succeeded in flattering a woman into luncheon at the Russian Tea Room, Sardi's, or La Goulue. Yet he was still vulnerable. He told me, "I have a little friend, a charming twenty-year-old Polish girl who studies medicine in New York. I go with her to concerts, lend her books, take her out to lunch. It is a harmless affair. The other day I had a little cold and she sent me one red rose. Being an old fogey, I cried."

With all the diversions and letters to women, books were his truest friends. He preferred the classics in any language and liked to poke fun at modern literature. He told me that once, while he was staying by invitation at a private estate in Palm Beach, Florida, he wandered into a big glitzy bookstore distinguished by its display racks of bestsellers. He came across a little paperback edition of *The Iliad,* picked it up, and said to it, "What are you doing here?"

With great literature at his fingertips, he could pull long excerpts out of his head for any occasion, and that would lead to unimagined tangents. Once, in a letter I wrote prior to taking a trip to Italy, I confided to Rudi how erotic I found the Italian language—even the affectation of an Italian accent from my husband when he was in an amorous and lighthearted mood. Rudi immediately replied:

> Of course! English is the ideal business language. Not a trace of eroticism. Even Shakespeare could not make it sexy. Take one of his sonnets, number 147, where he speaks of love:
>
> > *My love is a fever, longing still*
> > *For that which nurseth the disease,*

Feeding on that which doth preserve the ill,
Th' uncertain sickly appetite to please.

If Ernest can make this sound sexy, he is the wizard of language. But now take something Italian. For instance, Dante. Not something about love. No! Take the words written on the door of Hell (third canto) hinting at the most gruesome sights:

Per me si va nella città dolente;
per me si va nell' eterno dolore;
per me si va tra la perduta gente.

Let Ernest read this aloud and enjoy the sexy beauty of the *eterno dolore.* If you would not understand the words you might think that it is a confession of passionate love. What a pity you never had even a short, innocent flirt with an Italian boy. You would have a score of the most beautiful love letters, not necessarily because your friend was so passionate but because anything in Italian is full of passionate desire.

    I envy you your Italian trip. You will walk among memories of a civilization for which beauty had top priority. Today comfort has top priority. I end this letter with advice for Ernest: Whenever she is mad at you, tell her, "Don't bother me with your nonsense"—but say it with an Italian accent, and watch the result!

I wrote Rudi about my son's wedding, thinking he would be interested to know that my daughter-in-law had chosen an Emerson essay on love to be read at the ceremony. He wrote back:

Your daughter-in-law is certainly a lovely person but O—
my God to read aloud Emerson's boring essay on love to
wedding guests? Its appropriate subtitle should be "A Pu-
ritan's Ideas on Love." American writers are altogether not
very competent on love. They are great chasing the white
whale and trying to find out for whom the bells toll. But
love? Tell your daughter-in-law to read Stendhal's "De
l'amour." It is a masterpiece.

Rudi's quirky knowledge and use of literature to make his points included a ridiculous list of misogynistic quotations by Euripides,
Aristophanes, and various and sundry French thinkers from Proud-
hon to Baudelaire. I knew he thought he was being clever, but it
was infantile and annoying, and I let him have it:

Rudi, if you insist on quoting French and Greek misogy-
nists from here and there, you will dispel my former impression that you are a rare bird who appreciated the
wonders of women. As for me, there are only a very few
men worth regaling, and it is a very exclusive fraternity.

Your piano is safe and sound here, but it will be a
month before the technician gets it into tip-top shape.
Until then, alas, I will only be able to admire its pretty
shape and not hear its voice, which is probably all your
male philosophers want to do with women! Which brings
us full circle. With love . . .

He wrote back: "You are adorable when you let your tempera-
ment and convictions come through." He was sexist and elitist,
two traits I usually abhor, but he was so thoroughly dear, and
made me feel lovable.

I had become convinced that Rudi would live forever, but he

was finally too lame to go out and withdrew entirely into his beloved classics. He could still jest, reflecting that he thanked his physician for keeping him alive twenty years more than he had deserved, but adding, "Of course, fifteen of those years I spent sitting in your office waiting for you to see me!"

Now whenever we visited him, his nurse led us to his room, where he was deep in concentration. Once it was Dante's *Inferno* in Hungarian; another time, Montaigne in French. Sometimes he requested that we put on a Mozart recording. He said he could no longer abide any other composer. (The older I get, the easier it is for me to understand that.)

The only other divertissements were his wheelchair sorties, sometimes to the museum ("A charming young woman will push me around the Museum of Modern Art in a wheel chair. Nothing new: women pushed me around all my life"). When weather permitted, his nurse took him for rides in the park—and that, alas, is what finished him. One afternoon, as the nurse was wheeling him down an inclined path, the wheelchair got away from her. When the runaway vehicle finally rammed into an impediment, Rudi's poor, frail, skeletally thin body was dumped into a heap onto the sidewalk. He never recovered from that horrible accident and was dead within days.

Our friendship was one of the happiest of my life, and his experience and wisdom seemed to corroborate the things I was finding out for myself. What I think my letters brought to Rudi was a challenge to the pessimism he so often expressed:

> You might wonder how I managed to keep my good
> humor throughout this disquieting century. I tell you the
> secret: I have been, all my life, a pessimist and it gave me
> every day a thrill to see my dire prognoses come true. Be-

lieve me, dear girl, in today's world one has to be a pessimist to get a kick out of life.

I believe the happy surprises in his life that *disproved* his pessimism gave him a much greater thrill and ultimately kept him alive.

My Birds

"**G**RANDMA, why do you obsess about birds so much?" my grandson Rollie once asked me.

"First tell me how you know the word *obsess*?" I replied.

"Well, everyone is always asking me why I obsess so much about Godzilla!"

Why do I love the birds, Rollie? I would have to admit to the escape they offer into their compelling world, and sometimes, when all the world seems bleak and disappointing, it is the birds that deliver my spirit back to me.

Anyone who comes to visit, as you sometimes do, Rollie, from halfway across the country, will surely experience our busily trafficked bird feeders, my exasperation when the crows are intimidating the red-tailed hawk perched in our yard or sitting in the birdbath, and my crusade to attract others to the wonders of the avian world. Your dad resisted my request to watch the red-bellied woodpecker just outside the window, chiding, "Mom, You're the bird-watcher, not me. Enjoy it. I don't really care which bird is on the feeder."

Undaunted, I asked him to spare a glance, and he favored me by turning around, exclaiming "Holy —-!" I hear the beautiful birdsongs over the phone from your Southern garden in Louisiana, and I sus-

pect that your cardinals, mockingbirds, and barred owls are piquing his interest. (Every type A person needs a few birds in his life.)

Aunt Kim had to wait until she and her husband moved into a townhouse with a garden in the back, where she awoke to the songs of birds, for her interest to be reawakened. She had been my secret sharer of thrushes during her girlhood, but New York City life severed her connection with birds for a while, unless you count pigeons and starlings, which I don't. I am an elitist when it comes to birds.

Grandpa Ernie, my closest companion in all things, including bird-watching, and I are the only two people we know personally who can sit motionless for hours and take it all in. Then the sweet secrets are revealed: from a pair of cardinals' tenderest ministerings to each other to the most violent rivalries. If we watch a robin tugging at a perfect, supple strand of dried grass, we will soon know the site of her nest; a blue jay's spiral ascent through the boughs and around the trunk of a spruce will unwittingly reveal his nest, no matter how circuitous and misleading he thinks he is. In the cloud of raspberry-colored crabapple blossoms, we had the privilege of watching Mrs. Flicker fashion a perfectly round hole in the one dead branch of the tree about seven feet off the ground. Then we saw the inevitable attack of the gangster-starlings, and I got my slingshot ready to fight Mother Nature. (Grandpa says she's my true mother.) The same afternoon we watched chickadees gathering beaks full of thatched grasses for their nests, looking like they had whiskers, then flying straight as an arrow into the tiny hole of a brand new birdhouse we had hung the day before. The resident male catbird skittered around the yard after an intruding male, while the female sat mewing in the forsythia near her nest. A string of brilliant yellow goldfinches were stacked up on the thistle-seed feeder, flitting like liquid gold: cadmium yellow, gamboge, or citron doesn't begin to describe the quality of yellowness set off by their jet-black wings. We hear their wee chirps and chatterings all about, but they are secreted in the blossoming trees except when they alight on a feeder, a sunflower, or even a fragile cosmos that dips with the weight of the little bird pecking on the seedhead.

The year's first oriole streaked by my line of vision: nature's most brilliant vermilion. All of this on the same exquisite spring day, and then I heard my favorite bird: the first thrush of the year.

We do seem to live in a bird sanctuary, Rollie. The other day I was scrambling an egg when I had the distinct sensation of being watched. I turned around and saw the great big red-tail, the largest North American hawk, sitting on the birdbath outside the window, spying on me! His head with its almost-360-degree rotation took in everything around him, but basically he was keeping tabs on me. Grandpa Ernie managed to get me my camera; I shut the flash off, put the telephoto lens on, and got some great shots of—him? ("Tommy" Hawk)—or her? ("Kitty" Hawk)—before he took off. He was pretty casual, but the cardinal and the red-bellied woodpecker are more skittish. Generally, we have observed that the birds with more brightly colored plumage are more fearful, possibly because their bright colors make them more vulnerable.

The morning the hawk appeared I was grateful for the noisy cawing of the crows, as they warned the resident birds that the hawk was on the prowl for nestlings. The crows, ever aggressive, vigilant, territorial, with their aeries high atop our tallest evergreens, act as the "guardian angels" of all the birds—and that's the first nice thing I have ever said about crows!

I believe this blessed pastime has been health-giving and has made us into ecstatics. Conversely, it is abrasive to have people visit our sacred screened porch and make a racket as though nothing at all is taking place there. The porch is like a shrine and a temple to the birds, and we wish to keep it that way. Someone once said that in order to see the birds, you have to become part of the silence.

This, then, is my avian heaven, but it is also tinged with great sorrow, for the more one observes and becomes a creature of nature, the more one is vulnerable to its tragedies. And so the rest of this tale is an apologia and plea for forgiveness to the pair of cardinals who inhabited the scramble of honeysuckle and bittersweet vines on the side of our house.

The sight of you struggling, Mrs. Cardinal, and the sheer force of your will to live will be with me always. I tell your story to expunge the terrible feelings of guilt that permeate my whole being.

I went into the garage and found you sticking to an awful gum-pad, put there for the mice. No mouse should ever have to suffer as you did, and so the pads are now gone. Too late. I should never have left the garage door open, and yet it often is when we do garden work and need to get our tools.

There you were, spread-eagled, your beautiful wings outstretched, one entirely glued to the pad, and your fluffy rosy belly and fragile feet entirely stuck, beyond disengaging. I came to you in despair, and would even have sacrificed my own hands to wrest you from your awful fate; I tried to peel your sweet little body off, but your feisty spirit made you scream and peck me violently, lest I even touch you, you poor little thing.

Maybe you came for the same spilled birdseed that attracts the rodents, or maybe the sinister folks who invented the gum-pad made it smell attractive to unwitting innocent creatures like you. Perhaps its shiny surface looked like water. Somehow you managed through sheer force of will to disengage part of yourself, leaving only one part of your already terribly damaged right wing and one leg still stuck. I wanted to help you, dear Mrs. Cardinal, so I came close to try to separate the remaining parts of you from the terrible glue; instead I scared you into turning suddenly, so that you stuck your whole sweet tortured body once again to the death-pad. Now your head and neck and breast and wings were stuck, and your high-pitched cries broke my heart in two. Your steadfast mate was beside himself with panic, chipping his alarm cry from a nearby branch. I wouldn't have blamed him had he swooped down and pecked my eyes out, even though my heart has held nothing but love for you ever since you both nested in our hedge and fed from our feeders. That was me feeding you, don't you know?

I tried to slide a sharp flat tool between your breast and the pad in a last effort to try anything that might work, and you grabbed it in your beak with a force I could hardly believe was still in you after almost two hours of struggle. And then I saw what you were truly dealing with: your downy breast feathers had all been stripped from your belly, and your wounds were ripped open. I knew, even if you did not, that you would not make it, pretty little bird, and I was desperate to help you. I called the Volunteers for Wildlife and a lady told me what to do, the hardest thing I ever did. I filled a pail with water. Please understand I did this for you so your struggle would not last and last over hours filled with pain and suffering. I took you, irrevocably adhered to the ugly black pad, flapping, crying, confused, and I put you into the water. I did it with so much love, dear little thing, even as I trembled with the shock of it. I watched you gasp and gasp, I marveled at your will and strength, and I was with you until you could gasp no more. Tonight I will bury you so that no crow nor cat nor raccoon will disturb your sweet sleep. And I know your wish would be, with mine, that your mate find another with whom to complete the nest you must already have woven and prepared in the thicket. Or maybe you would rather have him mourn in solitude, in memory of your monogamous love over the past few years.

You were lovely on the snow, and on the holly bush. You were beautiful among the blossoming forsythia just this morning. Your tender loving care of each other was an inspiration—what any couple should be, and we will never forget you.

I heard the male cardinal sing all night, and for several nights thereafter, with a poignancy I had never heard before. I went about my work with deep sadness, until one day, a week later, a red flash caught my eye out the window. Surreptitiously I watched as the male cardinal courted a new female, magically arrived from the outside world to our garden. Soon she was carrying her own contributions to weave into the nest in the thicket. With her new mate's healing came my own, and with a bit of trepidation for what I might ever behold again, I went out to the porch

Summer Fest

THE superb evening concert at the Marlboro festival unleashed a whole gamut of emotions. The next day, in the
shade of a crooked old apple tree, to the music of a song sparrow
and the aroma of fermenting fruit, I reflected on the experience.
The purity of the musical event had been enhanced by the infor-
mality of the setting, including the artists' careless garb (except
for the Asian women performers, who were dressed to perfection). I had been exhilarated by the excellence of the ensembles,
some moving compositions written by Holocaust victims, and the
fierce emotionality of the African-American mezzo's interpretation of Ravel's *Madagascar Songs*.

But it was the final Beethoven "Ghost" Trio that had brought
me close to tears, not because it was so beautiful, nor beautifully
played, which it was, but because, I had to admit, *I* wasn't playing it. Generally I was able to feel an "episode" coming on and
rationalize myself back into sheer enjoyment by reminding myself of my choices; that is to say, that many years earlier I had
chosen a path that enabled me to raise a family, write, paint,
homemake, *and* play the piano publicly whenever the spirit
moved me. I did not, as I often insisted to myself and to others,

wish to wake up in Gopher Prairie one morning and Timbuktu the next, wherever my hypothetical tours would take me.

The reality was that this was beautiful Vermont, and there on the stage sat one of my former college classmates, now one of the most successful string players in the world; he and I had been the two most promising and frequent prizewinners on our campus.

Yes, the young pianist had played the trio well, and usually I rejoiced and reveled in young talent. But I felt the twinge, that immediately recognizable twinge of an emotion I would have deeply preferred not to admit to. Secretly I felt the shameful flush—no, the burn, igniting my blood, nourishing the notion that I might have brought more to the Beethoven trio, more ripeness and life, more humanness, more depth of experience. Then I chastised myself for those thoughts, and an inner discourse ensued: *No. There are many kinds of beauty. This was a younger, fresher Beethoven; on the other hand, this is Opus 70, not an early Beethoven. There are profound questions and answers here;* then finally, the dictum to myself: *Relax. Enjoy it.*

One of my deep regrets is that I never experienced the rarified atmosphere of a great music camp or summer festival as a youngster, because my nonmusician parents were not savvy about those things. While other gifted kids were auditioning and attending elite summer programs, I was wasting precious time and energy on what I considered mediocre pursuits. (For that reason, I take a more active role than my own teachers did in suggesting enriching summer courses for my gifted students.)

When I was about sixteen, I directed a production of *The Mikado* in a summer camp in upstate New York where my family owned a little cottage. I was really serving as the "Pooh-bah" (in *The Mikado,* Pooh-bah was the Lord High Everything Else); in other words, I was the music director, coaching everyone and running the rehearsals, dragging in scenery, accompanying the whole production, and so on, while my mother made the costumes and typed up everyone's scripts. My younger sister had the role of Pitti-sing, one of the "three little maids from school." In the end, I think we had quite a good production, considering our limited means and milieu. To this day I know every word of every patter song from *The Mikado*, not to mention the musical score. My mother, who has a genuine appreciation for the jolly wit of the libretto, also has vivid recollections of the production as a cozy family affair, and so she used to make frequent requests for me to "play *The Mikado*" when I visited. On those occasions, when their piano was in tune, I sat down, played the overture, and did an abbreviated impersonation of the characters, affecting a British accent; but it was as if I were an automaton. I was filled with the conflict between wanting to please her and my deep feeling of regret about the summers of my youth. The regret seemed to have compounded rather than dissipated over time as I realized the extent to which I had had to rely upon my own resources to invent productions such as these in order to create my own challenges.

Being asked to "play *The Mikado*" when I came to visit, when I would happily have played some Brahms intermezzi instead, had become, for me, a metaphor and a device. The operetta kept my pianistic ability within a family context: it was familiar, cute, and historic. But being reduced to a nickel-in-the-slot accompanist, while feeling discouraged about sharing the real essence and excitement of my professional life, out of a family ethic that suggests that talking about one's life and pleasures is showing off, worked together into an unpleasant sensation. So eventually I declined to rerun the show, feeling somewhat guilty but greatly relieved. More recently, I have sent some recordings of live performances for my parents to enjoy while I am not visiting, and *The Mikado* has receded into distant memory.

However, as I sat in the audience at Marlboro listening to the great Beethoven trio, my contrary mind insisted upon summoning up old disappointments and comparisons, rendering the contrast between the Beethoven trio and the youthful summer of Gilbert and Sullivan excruciating.

I glanced over at a hoary-headed pianist, also a listener. His body, too, was lurching with each *sforzando,* swaying in sympathy with each lyric phrase. His fingers, too, revealed spasms of ghost-playing. Perhaps every other pianist in the room, not only I, was "playing" or wishing to play the trio. Once a pianist . . .

During the intermission I spoke to the well-known older pianist, yet his eyes rarely met mine for darting glances around the room. At first this mannerism had seemed egocentric and rude, but when I realized the reason behind it, he became a rather sympathetic creature: he was hoping to be recognized in the crowd, and possibly he was searching to see if there were any folks who were more politically advantageous around, to whom he might be speaking—anyone who could engage him for one more gig or next summer's festival. To watch someone over sixty hustling was sad, whereas I could acknowledge that I was generally quite contented with my lot. Only once in a while, a dark cloud of ambiguity cast shadows on my generally happy musical life. At times like this, I forced an inventory of my blessings, a kind of litany by now: a terrific second marriage to a man who knew how to live and let live; gifted, bright children and grandchildren; beautiful home and garden; friends; and aged parents still miraculously here. A beautiful world with no struggles. And a "Ghost" Trio at home or in a small hall with superb colleagues any time I wished to arrange it. I jumped to my feet to applaud the deserving players. Then I overheard two young resident-musicians complaining about their insect-infested cottages and was grateful to be returning to our luxurious mountain inn.

I realized a long time ago that I do not have the constitution for a touring life in music, that those choices I made were based on other needs—like the comforts of home and the luxury of spending my time as I wish without the constant pressure of a concert looming over me. Still, throughout the many years that have passed since I came to that fork in the road and chose to turn away from a life entirely devoted to the piano, I have had recurrent episodes of doubt and sadness such as the one in Vermont. Most of these have occurred in concert halls when I hear disappointing performances by artists that fall short of my own standards and expectations. At times like those, the only cure for me has been to plan a concert of my own. And so it has been that over the years, I have never stopped playing and have somehow managed to establish a scaled-down career without sacrificing anything.

Within weeks of my visit to the Vermont music festival, I got two consecutive telephone calls. According to the laws of synchronicity, nothing in the universe occurs without a reason. The first call occurred at eleven o'clock at night. A man inquired whether he was speaking to Carol Montparker. Before replying, out of my semisomnolent state, I asked his name and he gave it readily. It rang some distant bell from my youth, and when I identified myself, he yelped, "I can't believe I have found you! I was Nanki-poo in your production of *The Mikado* at camp!"

Over forty years later I was apparently being hunted down simply because that modest little production of the operetta had made deep and lasting impressions on its cast members. They had even, apparently, all assembled for a little reunion in that tiny upstate New York community where it all had taken place. According to "Nanki-poo," now a professor of genetics at a university in the Midwest, they were all asking, "I wonder where Carol is now?"

This is how I learned that I not only had left my mark where I had no clue of having done so, but had snobbishly denied and dismissed something of value from my past that had been cherished by others, including my own mother.

The next call was the first of several in the succeeding months from David Dubal, pianist, author, and inspired host of a wonderful program, "Reflections from the Keyboard." The program features piano music in comparative performances and is aired on WQXR, *The New York Times* FM radio station. He had heard my CD and phoned to say, "I am putting you on with the immortals!" He told me he would play an excerpt from my recording next to the same piece played by another pianist.

When the first designated evening came, I suddenly became unusually nervous. I asked myself whether my own Chopin interpretation would stand up alongside those by renowned pianists. I knew in my heart that if I had not believed there was value in my playing, I never would have enshrined it forever in the vinyl of the CD. Dubal often critiques the various selections presented on the air; it's his program, after all, and he is a leading expert on piano music. What if, I asked myself, he doesn't like my playing and pans it on the air? *Well then*, the answer came up in my head, *that is only one man's opinion.*

In the end, my recording was played right after the interpretation of a giant in piano history, William Kapell, and it seemed to fare very well, thanks to the positive responses of the host. The next morning I realized that the bit of recognition on a public classical music radio station was a defining moment in my musical life. I was the only nonfamous person on that program. Every other pianist, dead or alive, had taken the right fork in the road, while I had taken the left. All had devoted their entire lives to careers as concert pianists, while I had had the luxury of raising a family, writing, painting an occasional watercolor, digging in the dirt in my garden, and still performing whenever I wanted to. Yet for those few moments, I was "in the club," introduced as "the American-born pianist, Carol Montparker."

Rubinstein, Michelangelo, and Ernest

I NEVER expected to be invited to Arthur Rubinstein's ninety-fifth birthday bash, but there was the invitation in the mail: black-tie dinner to be held at the Waldorf Astoria Grand Ballroom. As a member of the press I reviewed concerts for *Clavier*, wrote feature stories, and did interviews; occasionally a plum of an event like this one came up to justify all the hard work. I knew exactly what I would wear, but Ernie had no tux. We could justify neither renting nor buying one, so we went around to a couple of thrift shops and found a really good pair of tux pants exactly his tall size—but no jacket. A friend suggested we make the rounds of tailor shops, where one can sometimes buy garments that have gone unclaimed. Happily, Michelangelo, the Italian tailor, had a decent-looking jacket that fit Ernie pretty well. We splurged on a brand new cummerbund and bow tie and thought we looked pretty good when we left for the city that evening. Our high expectations, though, were peppered with some doubts as to whether the ancient pianist would actually show up.

Moments after we were seated at a table with other journalists, it was announced that Rubinstein was too feeble to attend. There would be reminiscences by friends and a video of a recent interview of him in an apartment in Switzerland. The news was not surprising, and an air of celebration prevailed nevertheless. Listening to his reflections in person or on tape was a major event. He was a bon vivant, a great raconteur, and a joker, and he could mold his elastic, expressive face to suit the mood of the moment. He spoke of the fact that he had no hobbies, only passions—for books, paintings, travel, food, cigars. He recounted tales of friendships with Picasso, Casals, Piatigorsky, Stravinsky, Falla, Granados, Poulenc, Ravel, Golda Meir, Gandhi; his eyes, though nearly blind, sparkled with his undying lust for life. There were some clips of his performances, distinguished by his unmistakable, gorgeous, round, sonorous tone, and as he played the camera closed in on his face, devoid of the frivolity of the storyteller; he was the least sentimental and the most straightforward and honest when he was at the piano. His spirit was strongly present at the party.

The next time Ernest decided to wear a tux was five years later for a senior prom at his high school, and this time he was determined to buy a new one. We danced the entire night, and the next day the tux was sent to Michelangelo the tailor for cleaning, after which it hung for another five years in the back of Ernest's closet.

We do not belong to a jet-setting, glitterati, upper-crust crowd. Our lives, if measured by black-tie events, may be judged plebeian, humble, even humdrum. And so it was that when we were invited to a black-tie wedding of our friends' son at a fancy club in Manhattan, Ernie fished around in the back of his closet, took out his tux, and decided to send it again to Michelangelo for cleaning a few days before the wedding. We got dressed late in the afternoon in order to leave for the city at six o'clock.

At about five-thirty, my handsome husband asked, "How do I look?"

I looked him over, and somehow he looked all wrong.

"What's the matter with your tux?" I asked.

"What do you mean, 'What's the matter?'" he replied.

"Your shirt cuffs are sticking out. It's too small on you!"

"No. This is my tux. This is how it's supposed to fit."

"No, Ernie. It's a couple of sizes too small on you. They either shrank the tux at the cleaners, or they gave you back the wrong suit. We have to call Michelangelo immediately. Maybe he hasn't closed yet."

We looked up the number frantically, and I got on the phone with Michelangelo.

"Mr. Michelangelo, this is Ms. Montparker. There is something quite wrong with my husband's tux. I think you gave him the wrong one. It is two inches too short in the sleeves."

"No, Missus. I no give heem the wrong one. Eetsa hees tux. I no have no odder tuxes thisa week."

"Mr. Michelangelo, it fit him fine the last time he wore it. You must have shrunk it then."

Michelangelo's voice got angrier. "I no shrinka de tux. Eetsa *dry* cleaning!"

It was getting too late to haggle, so I said goodbye and hung up. I looked at my poor husband who, by now, had beheld himself in the full-length mirror with a bit of horror. We had to leave the house right then or miss the wedding ceremony. I advised him to try to loosen his belt and drop his pants a bit, and to try to walk around withdrawing his arms back into his sleeves to the extent he could, so he wouldn't look like a pauper relative expecting a flood. Several times throughout the evening my silent signals to him triggered a strange contortion causing the shrinkage of his wrists inside the sleeves, but as the wedding photos subsequently revealed, he looked like a misfit. Eventually, though, after two or three martinis, neither of us cared any more.

We returned home in the wee hours of the night, and as we were undressing, I heard a weird howl. "Oh my God!" Then strange cackling, halfway between laughter and an asthmatic attack. "Come here, Carol. Here's my good tux."

He retrieved his excellent designer tux in its plastic dry-cleaners bag from the rear of the closet. "That was the old thrift-shop tux I got for the Rubinstein party ten years ago that I wore tonight."

We laughed ourselves to sleep that night, and the next morning we chucked the miserable garment into a carton to bring to the thrift shop for some other pitiable—or at least smaller—victim to own someday.

Greta's Melody

THIS tale is a romance in which I played an oblique role. I have frequently made love matches between my piano students and certain pianos. I have cajoled estate auctioneers into parting with old instruments for less than their greedy little palms were itching for so that students might upgrade their pianos; I have even jumped in when someone I knew died to arrange for a student to "meet" a piano before it went on the open market. I have rescued neglected little uprights that were being put out at the curb for collection and found them homes with beginning piano students, and I have helped to persuade parents of gifted young students to go in somewhat over their heads, just as my parents did when I was young, to provide a lovely instrument that will inspire their child. Perhaps because one of my greatest pleasures has been my relationship with my own piano, I want to share the experience. Some folks might consider me controlling. I admit I have been in certain cases when I am certain I am doing good.

One day, Greta, a very pleasant, enthusiastic, and musical student asked me whether I thought she could play Franz Schubert's *Hungarian Melody*. I didn't really know the piece, so the next week she brought me a CD of Alfred Brendel playing some of the *Klavier-*

stücke along with the piece she wanted to learn. I quickly determined that she could, indeed, play it, and so she bought the music.

"I want to surprise my husband," she explained. "I will have to practice it when he is not at home. It's his favorite piece, and his birthday is in two months."

"What a charming idea. Let's get to work!" And so I began my complicit role in this delightful conspiracy.

Within the next two months she had mastered the lovely work almost as well as Brendel. In fact, with my usual proprietary feeling about the compositions I teach, I learned it too, and planned to program it in a group of Schubert works. I chanced to mention that I wished I could be present at the gift-giving ceremony to witness her husband's surprise, and so she forthwith invited Ernest and me to his birthday dinner. We did not know the couple socially, and I had only met her husband once or twice; but the invitation was too intriguing to pass up.

According to the plan, after dinner I was supposed to say, "Greta, I have never heard you play your piano. Would you play something for us?" We settled in the living room, and I think both she and I were a bit nervous and very anxious that she play her best. I noticed that her Yamaha upright was positioned in back of her husband's easy chair. This meant that Greta would be facing the piano and the wall and therefore unable to experience the full impact of the scenario we had set up. But Greta is a modest and unassuming woman. She is profoundly hard of hearing, but has overcome the handicap with the use of her hearing aids and a highly developed sense of touch. In addition, she has an excellent ear (a faculty and talent related to musicality and altogether *un*related to hearing). She has a whole palette of tonal colors to draw from, and no one would ever guess she was in any way disabled when she plays. Greta has none of the performer's vanities; her only aim was to give the gift of this beautiful music from her hands and heart to her husband's ears. They have a tasteful and beautiful home and a very well-behaved, handsome standard poodle named Jacques, whose alert posture seemed to reflect a sense of event.

I recited the cue, and of course Greta agreed, going to the piano somewhat tentatively. Greta has no guile, and she has the ability to concentrate. As soon as she began to play the introductory bass figure, I knew it would go well. The sound of ego and conviction was in her hands and she meant to do her best. No one was watching Greta. We were watching her husband, Bill. His face first reflected benign expectation of some familiar piece, then momentary bewilderment, the bittersweet flicker of recognition, and finally a supreme effort to control his deep emotions. He knew this music well, but not from his wife's hands and heart; and when the impact hit him of all the love and time and devoted hard work it must have taken her to prepare this monumental surprise for him, he was just about overwhelmed.

She finished her mini-recital and got up, unprepared to see three teary listeners dabbing at their eyes. She, too, was overcome with emotion and stepped behind her husband, putting her hand on his shoulder. He got up and hugged her, and it was a mighty pretty sight. In a world full of stress and misery, encounters with true enduring love are rare and precious.

The following week, Greta came for her lesson illuminated by a momentous bit of news: Bill had decided to buy her a grand piano and was doing some research on the subject of piano manufacturers. They chose an Austrian-made Schimmel and waited several months for it to arrive from Europe. It's a gorgeous-looking instrument, and from my vantage point, it has enhanced their living room, their relationship, and certainly her playing.

Healing House

I SURVEY the room every so often out of disbelief. Everything I love has its own carefully chosen place. The two pianos cuddle neck in neck, a massive paisley shawl covering their two bodies. Nearby on a library table is a collection of photos: one of myself at around forty, freshly divorced, radiantly happy; photos with family, with luminaries I interviewed for *Clavier*, favorite students; candid shots with my children; romantic ones with Ernest; pictures of chamber music colleagues, my teacher, my parents, and group classes of my students—altogether a rather unabashedly narcissistic and thoroughly satisfying hodgepodge.

The photo taken outside Carnegie Recital Hall after my long-postponed solo recital reflects the joy of feeling like the most important person in New York City that night—black velvet gown, coterie of friends and family, headlights streaming by, illuminated marquee, poster announcing my concert alongside the entranceway. Goodness knows there are concerts at Carnegie every single evening, and in every other hall in the city, simultaneously; yet, for me, that evening generated a surreal, heightened awareness, and an exquisite tension that I can still muster up whenever I think back. Thankfully, my ex-husband captured all the excitement on film. Now when I regard those photos I wonder how I ever managed to work and achieve my goal with a personal life in such disarray.

On the wall are wonderful paintings. All my life I have had artist-friends who have been as generous in spirit as they tell me I have been with my music. A few of the paintings were left to me by my great teacher, Leopold Mittman: he and I always shared a love of painting as well as musical ideas. The glorious, lively Tibetan rugs, colored with vegetable dyes, are slowly fading in certain sunbathed swaths, further enhancing their beauty.

Sun drenches the room; that was one of the prerequisites when we moved here thirty years ago. When I was finally living here alone I could fully appreciate the house's beauty. The walls no longer echoed rancorous shouts and curses; the sun and rain and freedom had washed them all away. This cottage abuts a woodland tract that I pray will never be developed. It is not a big house, but the low-hung windows bring the outdoors in. People refer to it as "the yellow house" on our road, but the shingles are more the color of winter meadow grasses, and the shutters are the dark green of the wild cedar that spring up in the middle of undeveloped fields.

I had gone straight from my father's house into an early marriage that was not meant to be, yet lasted much too long. For the first time in my life, after the divorce, I would be on my own, and I had more elation than fear or trepidation for the prospect. The notion of having total aesthetic control over my environment and complete prerogative over my whole life made me euphoric. Even the smallest decisions gave me enormous delight: years earlier I had had to abide angry dicta, for example, that I "may not hang the wash on a line to dry in the sun, and turn the place into a shantytown." The fresh smell of sun-dried laundry is one of my great delights. So my first act of independence was to go out and buy clothesline and wooden clothespins, suspend the rope between two posts, and hang an entire United Nations of colored towels, that felt like triumphant freedom banners, out to fly and dry in the brilliant sun.

I knew I would have to teach more than I truly wished to, to teach pupils I might otherwise not have accepted, and to hustle for playing gigs to bring in as much income as I could muster; economic disaster was one of my recurring nightmares. And thus I embarked on a new episode, making a conscious decision never to marry again, but not to abandon the possibility of romance. In the first year or two there were several friendships that crossed the boundaries into brief intimacy, sweet encounters, but no great love that threatened my resolve to stay single and live my life alone. I was never lonely. I love to be alone. I had memorable correspondences: the daily mail was one of the high points of my existence, often bringing me loving, fascinating letters from exotic places. I even had letters from friends in town who, like me, preferred to write rather than phone. (I still prefer the pleasure of handwritten missives to the phone or e-mail.) Whenever I wanted to I went to the city for concerts and museum shows, and life was deeply satisfying.

My days began early with a walk with my dog. The only carry-over from my former life was Polly, the dearest mutt that ever walked the earth. She accompanied me wherever I went, including to the piano, where she lay contentedly near the pedals until I was done practicing. Two hours of hard work on repertoire from nine to eleven in the morning in an empty house (unless you count Polly) resounded with a sense of more purpose and fulfillment than ever before. The rest of the day was divided among errands, teaching, writing, the garden, and staring into space—a good balance between unstructured and productive time.

One day the relatively short solitary spell in my life came to an end. My old friend Nelly, a Viennese refugee from Hitler's Europe, invited me to a party where I met a man unlike any other man I had ever known. Nelly's house was where I had escaped to during certain intolerable times in my first marriage, but that day Nelly morphed from confidante into fairy godmother. She was a friend with whom I could talk about everything: bird watching, ballet, classical music, gardens, and love, all with equal enthusiasm. Nelly was a very wise woman. She was the one who advised me that instead of lamenting my ex-husband's extramarital escapades, I should make it easy for him to have yet one more affair so that my divorce would be a clear-cut case. And that was the way I got to the end of a long, tortuous tunnel.

At this particular party, euphemistically arranged to celebrate Memorial Day, she had in mind that I meet a friend of hers who had lost his wife at about the same time my marriage had ended. Someone asked me to play something on the piano; I think I played the "Pathétique" Sonata by Beethoven, and I distinctly remember the feeling of being regarded intently by a tall lean man with horn-rimmed glasses, a sensitive, intelligent face, and a hearty laugh. I remember little else of that afternoon, except a deep longing to take a walk with him—no unreasonably romantic goal, just a walk. That nagging notion lasted several days until, miraculously, he phoned me.

"I wondered whether you'd be interested in a piano recital that is taking place at my school this week?"

"Are you going?"

"No, I can't make it, but I thought you might like to go."

"Well, thanks for letting me know," I responded, and that was the whole conversation. *What a jerk!* I thought. *Why would I want to go alone to a concert at his school?* I was terribly disappointed, but the truth is that we were both so out of practice in the rites of courtship after our long respective marriages that that was the best excuse he could think of to call.

But the next day he called again and asked me whether I would like to take a walk on the beach. Since that day I have believed in psychic phenomena. We walked and talked as easily as if we had known each other for years. His lean tallness, the crisp, clean smell of his cotton shirt, his funny boyish sneakers on his outsized feet, and the way I fit under his arm when he put it around me was so comfortable and amiable. We walked some more, holding hands that felt galvanized, and a bit further down the beach he stopped, I stopped, and he bent down to kiss me.

I remarked something like "that kind of kiss is at least a third-date kiss"; we laughed and walked some more. Since that walk on the beach, we have been with each other every day of our lives.

On our first wedding anniversary, Ernest gave me a necklace that reflected the wonder and joy we both found in life with each other. It was fashioned from odd bits of old Bohemian glass beads, shaped like flowers and shells, that seemed to swing and dance happily on tiny links suspended from a delicate chain. The exquisite colors, some subtly opaque as beach glass, some clear as prisms, reminded me of my dappled gardens, of fresh watercolors sparkling on wet paper, of clotheslines hung with vivid banners. Ernie's little card that accompanied the gift began with his poem, "Heaven sits on your toes," and was dedicated, "this wildflower necklace to a wildflower beauty from your loving bee."

The necklace was too beautiful to put inside a drawer. When I was not wearing it, I hung the strand of crystals in front of our bedroom window to allow the sunlight to filter through and throw sprays of colored speckles all over the walls. Once or twice I sat and peered at the world through fragments of rose, amethyst, emerald, or ruby glass. I often contemplated the gift of timing that brought us together. Generally we believed in letting go of the past, even with its uncanny parallels in our respective earlier years.

Once we made the decision, we lived comfortably in this relatively small house. My excellent dog had to make accommodations with this new arrangement, but I think she knew that all the changes were right.

The most curious surprise was the musical bond between us. The myth of a two-musician marriage being made in heaven had been shattered daily in my other life. As an educator and administrator with a focus on literature and poetry, Ernest and I brought to each other miracles of art that neither of us hitherto had had time to explore. I was not ashamed to ask him basic questions about Shakespeare plays with which I yearned to become intimate; and he was unabashedly in awe of the piano. He would sometimes sit quite close to watch my fingers or the hieroglyphics on the page in the hopes of gaining some comprehension of the mysteries. I played beautifully for him because his intuitions and musicality were constantly astounding to me, even though his understanding was limited. He scat-sang à la Ella Fitzgerald in the shower, embroidering around melody in a way that very few can do, and his musical memory was astute.

One afternoon after I had finished playing a Chopin piece, Ernest asked, "How would you like to go over to that field we passed the other day and dig out some lupines you've been eyeing for your garden?" If someone had plumbed my psyche to discover the most perfect and ideal way to spend the next few hours, that would have been it.

A half-hour later I was tramping through the low-growing thicket, menaced by redwings whose territories I was challenging, while Ernie sat in the car reading. (I hadn't expected that he help me dig out the plants. This was my project, and he had no interest in doing it. I had lost none of my independence. What I had gained is someone who supported it.) For years I had watched this neglected tract grow wilder and wilder, swallowing up what must once have been a nursery or a great garden; and now, armed with a bucket, spade, boots, and a special energy—born of happiness, I think—I dug around the plants, lifting them with a clump of soil big enough to allow them to be rescued safely to my garden.

Trudging back toward the car, I could hear the radio with strains of Brahms's First Symphony and Ernie's wonderful voice singing out without any self-consciousness, his arms waving like a maestro's. I could not have felt more connected to any so-called professional musician. Back at home, Ernie brought me a portable radio with the end of the Brahms: music to plant by, while he went out to do some errands. I brought a pail of compost, dug a deep hole, and tamped the soil down around the lupines, coming up for air when the plants were safely nestled in my garden. Leaning back on my shovel, somewhat alarmed at the rapid beating of my heart, I took a deep breath, looked up to watch a red-tailed hawk circling overhead, and made my way over to the porch to contemplate how life can sometimes be so perfect.

Then Ernie underwent heart surgery, and all the perfection was shattered for a while. One day as he was recovering (and as I was recovering from my post-traumatic stress syndrome), he watched from the patio as I satisfied my overwhelming impulse to plant a few rosebushes to celebrate his survival. Gardening, even more than music, restored my spirit, and I was in a state of ecstatic gratitude.

It was the wonderful month of May, and our anniversary was coming up.

Ernie asked me, "What would you like to have, Carol? I'd like to get you a pair of diamond earrings. Would you like that?"

"Ernie, you want to get me stones? Then get me *real* stones: Pennsylvania river stones, a whole palette of them, delivered to our garden."

I love what the Japanese say about their gardens: that the rocks represent permanence, and the plants represent change. A perfect balance, not to mention the beautiful juxtaposition of plants with stone.

Shortly thereafter not one but two pallets of stones—two tons, to be exact—were dumped in a sort of fallen-Stonehenge mountain in one corner of our property. The river stones are softened around the edges from eons of water corrosion; they feel almost soft to the touch when you run your hands over the rounded contours. The rocks were gorgeous, both together and each by itself, and I realized that I could not have wished for anything more beautiful. Each had its own vibration, almost its own voice.

I stood there contemplating the magnitude of the acquisition, and set forth alone while my stupefied husband watched me, lifting them, one by one, with a brute strength I never knew I had, motivated by gratitude and gladness. One person's definition of gardening is digging holes and pouring money into them. For me, the magic and the wonder is that you can break your neck and your back, herniate yourself, burst blood vessels in your eyeballs, and render your hands useless at the piano by lifting more than your body was ever meant to, and still the results yield utter peace.

I created steppingstones between the clumps of perennials, stone paths, and low stone walls, albeit uneven, crude ones, everywhere. A person can never have enough rocks, and after a month of harder physical labor than I'd ever done, I looked around me and saw something like an English country landscape. Particularly interesting chunky rocks were placed strategically as accents in the garden. On the north shore of Long Island where we live, indigenous rocks that were deposited during the Ice Age are scattered here and there in woods and fields, like wildflowers. I found one huge boulder shaped like a dinosaur's egg in the woods and rolled it, inch by inch, like a crazed cavewoman, over half an acre to a chosen spot in the garden. It looked like it had rolled and come to rest there all by itself.

I still had about half a ton of stones left, so I began building a conical structure, wide at the base and narrowing as it rose. It was as though I had been inhabited by a prehistoric ghost. The result was a stone cairn: a folly, as the English call their fanciful, phantasmagoric configurations with no real function except to delight or mystify. I felt it to be related to the ancient cairns one sees all over Europe: a shrine? a marker? an icon to love? It is positively useless and utterly beautiful, like the Druidic fantasies that motivated ancient man to create stone circles and towers with found stone.

I have come to know two truths about myself: that I love to create beautiful things, and that I love to challenge myself. I actually even love the physical exertion and, in the end, the sense of attaining a serenity I had never known before, working, resting, purveying the accomplishment, wondering at the great beauty everywhere. I gaze at the stone walls that were put together in what felt to me like meaningful juxtapositions, and I notice the irregularities; sometimes I juggle the pieces or fill in the gaps with smaller shards, but generally I like the randomness that appears in the natural world itself.

The spring following the stone projects, we had our bluestone entrance patio torn up and replaced with sandstone and limestone blocks. The flat bluestones were dumped onto the leftover river stones. Chipmunks had by then adopted the tower for their "city" residence, as I told my grandchildren, and Rollie and Zoe decided to build another cairn, not far from my folly. I stepped aside and watched them, like me, lifting, considering, discarding, or selecting each stone, gaining in appreciation and excitement for both the materials and the results. A few months later, another grandson, Steven, got right into the spirit building his own tower, while his sisters, Linda and Julia, watched. How superior to the box of playing blocks we usually lugged out.

I love to watch our five grandchildren experience the beauty of the elements of nature. If I make no other contribution to their lives, I want them to have my curiosity and wonder for the natural world.

The house has changed very little in the last twenty years. Without exception, students and friends have always responded happily to our environment. It is a kind of wonderland, a piano-garden of delight into which we only invite people whom we experience harmoniously in the space, and who would appreciate or at least respect its balance and beauty. Occasionally I have had to whisk out, fast, anyone—a parent of a student or an acquaintance—who seems totally discordant here. It was in this controlled environment that I had originally regained my feeling of self after a long and damaging marriage. I recently heard the poet Maya Angelou say the same thing about her house. If she hears a prejudiced or negative word from a guest, she escorts them to the door. "Words are *things,*" she said. "They are absorbed by the walls and the furniture and the food, and they can toxify the environment. My house is a *healing house.* Folks come here to experience positive energy and joy." Her words might have been uttered by me.

Apparently the ambience and aura that surround the place are far-reaching. Friends from Oregon who were planning to visit us for the first time went into a shop prior to their departure. They chanced to mention their upcoming trip "to Long Island," and when the salesperson asked what town, they responded, "Huntington."

"Where in Huntington? I used to live in the next town, Centerport !" she exclaimed.

Our friends mentioned the name of our road.

"I know exactly where that is! There's a yellow house I always loved, way back from the road. I always wanted to live there."

CD Collection

MY knees were locked, my back was sore, and my brain was spinning: I realized that I had sat absolutely motionless for several hours listening to some CDs I had received that day. These were no ordinary CDs I had bought or received as gifts. They were not the freebies I have been sent over the years by public-relations firms promoting young artists, nor were they the CDs of famous artists I had admired all the years of my musical life. But I was surprised to acknowledge secretly to myself—who else could I acknowledge this to?—that these CDs were every bit as respectable as the interpretations I had heard either live from famous artists, or bought, or had sent to me. They were *my* CDs: recordings from live concerts past, rescued from decaying cassettes or reel-to-reel tapes. I had been paying expert audio technicians over the last few months to resurrect whatever they could from varying stages of deterioration before my past slipped soundlessly, irreversibly away.

It occurred to me that if I were a visual artist, my paintings would survive me, just as books survive a writer. But musical performances are so ephemeral. A note is struck and seconds later it is dead. Over. *Fini.* A concert is performed, and it ends with no trace that it ever happened, except in the vague realm of memory. Daniel Barenboim once said that being a musician prepares you for death.

You are constantly reminded, with everything you play, that your music vanishes with the moment, and that very quality of transience is what makes it ever more precious, just as a flower is made more beautiful by its impermanence, just as life itself is so dear because it is finite. I have played many concerts that were never recorded, and except for a tattered program, I have almost no sense of those events; but I did still have a considerable number of concert tapes lying around in drawers. It frightened me to find that they were slowly disintegrating; I felt as though a vital part of me was falling away, and that soon there would be no trace of the work and achievement of my past musical life.

I had a few deep thoughts on the subject of the preservation of art for the future after seeing the extraordinary documentary *Rivers and Tides,* about the work of the Scottish artist Andy Goldsworthy, who makes constructions in nature using only natural materials: grasses, branches, rocks, sand, leaves, even ice. His work is meant to be ephemeral and is soon washed away with the tide or blown by the winds. The temporal status of his pieces only adds to their preciousness.

Still, I mentioned my fears regarding the vaporizing of the music into thin air to my former student Howard, who has been like another son to us for the past ten years. He asked me to "lend" him a few of my best reel-to-reel tapes from the past, and before I knew what was happening, and to my great surprise and delight, for my birthday I received from him a packet of CDs, beautifully remastered and transformed into wonderful listening experiences for me: the Brahms D Minor Concerto, the Schumann A Minor Concerto, and my entire Carnegie Recital Hall program, all rescued and permanently preserved. It was one of the greatest gifts I have ever received. And so I embarked on a continuation of the rescue project he began and have slowly accumulated a whole shelf of CD jewel boxes filled with millions of tones from solo recital programs, concerto performances, joint concerts with my son and daughter; and I think to myself, *Not a bad body of work.*

But as I listened to the latest batch in my collection, my brain began spinning with questions. *Why is this so important to me? Why do I get so sad and at the same time so happy when I listen to them? Why am I so disappointed even as I feel so grateful? Who will ever hear these CDs? Am I enough for myself? What was so fascinating about my younger self at the piano that I sat so riveted to one spot listening? Where did the years go? How have I changed? How would I play those masterworks differently with all these years of added perspective?*

The sadness is comparable to anyone contemplating lost time. In my case, those years were not my happiest, and the music I made was born more of struggle than the peace I have now. Music was my refuge, much more than it is now, and listening to those performances, I am stunned at the mere fact of their existence, of the resilience and drive that persisted despite the exigencies of my personal life. At the same time, I am reminded that as tense as life was at home, some of those tapes were recorded by my ex-husband; thus, although he took away the major part of my youth, he unwittingly gave an important portion of it back to me with those tapes. Unfortunately, the recordings he made are amateurish, so I can still hear his coughing, his breathing, his clapping, to bring me back to the realities of those days.

My readings of the Brahms intermezzi are impetuous and I know I would play them with more breadth and introspection now; but I understand and even like the ardent, youthful pianist in those concerts. Could I still rattle off some of the virtuosic works with as much abandon? Yes, but I wouldn't want to. I am working on literature I didn't touch in those days—Schubert sonatas and *lieder* with a wonderful bass-baritone, late Beethoven, and Ravel.

I thought I was investing in this project for my children, so they would have a musical legacy from me, so that one day, long after I am gone, they might find the moments to sit down and listen and share what I had to say musically. But, curiously, that doesn't matter as much to me now. I think my main motive was to have the music available to myself. Certainly I was not planning to market any of the recordings commercially. There are tiny flaws here and there, barely perceptible slips, maybe one or two per concert, that might fly by, unmarked, in a concert setting. These were spontaneous human accounts rendered in front of live audiences, with all the coughs and crinkling lozenge wrappers to prove it—but these very proofs render the recordings unfit for a market that insists on the perfection of cut-and-paste studio takes. Our ears have been spoiled by miraculous technology that produces laundered results.

I am my own worst critic, and the odd slip at the time of the concerts was difficult to tolerate. But retrospect and maturity have afforded me a comfortable sense of forgiveness. Besides, there is nothing to excuse, in my opinion; if there were, I wouldn't want to share the CDs with colleagues and friends. As with a watercolor, the result of a recital might not be exactly what an artist had planned. We take risks and meet with happy surprises, moments of improvisation that surprise even ourselves. There are so many variables—the hall, the piano, the audience, our physical and emotional health, the time of day—how could we ever predict the exact way we will play? We have intentions, but sometimes even better alternatives present themselves right in concert. It is only with the perspective of time that we can truly know how successful a piece of work has been.

My son, Dennis, a superb cellist, is now the age I was when many of these recitals took place, and I have salvaged some of the concerts we gave jointly. These recordings I could listen to for hours, as they contain some of the deepest communication we have ever shared. They are incredible documents of playing that hardly ever had to be discussed. Genetic consensus took over and yielded amazing results.

My son and I have a rather Mendelssohnian relationship, by which I mean that our music expresses more than we have been able to put into words. Mendelssohn once said that while most people consider music too abstract and words a much more defined means of communication, for him it was completely the opposite: music more exactly expressed thoughts and feelings. Certainly Dennis and I resorted to music in many a situation when words failed us—for example, the evening before he left for his first year of college, when we said goodbye with a deeply felt reading of Beethoven's great Sonata for Cello and Piano in A Major, Opus 69. Ever since then, he has lived far away from me— halfway across the United States, or as far away as South America, coming home for brief visits during which our attempts at catching up on news and feelings or at recapturing a smooth, unfettered flow of ideas can sometimes be hard. When the spoken word has been too arduous, one or the other of us has simply asked, "Want to play?" And then the pent-up emotions and unresolved conversations have seemed to straighten themselves out.

Dennis is a thorough professional with a different perspective than mine, and he will find it hard to abide the little imperfections in the CDs that I will want to share. I yearn to sit down quietly and listen together—not to talk, just to listen to the music speaking what we had to say years ago, when, even though his parents' marriage was falling apart, he and I were still able to make beautiful music, Bach, Beethoven, César Franck, Brahms, Falla.

My daughter, Kim, is a successful textile designer who could still make a career in flute if she wanted to. She and I played our hearts out on many occasions, but one incredible CD of her senior flute recital, on the stage of her high school auditorium with hundreds of people listening, was a minor miracle. There sat her father, from whom I had recently separated, recording our program: Bach Sonata for Flute and Harpsichord in A Major, Beethoven Serenade, Poulenc Sonata, Bolling jazz pieces, Debussy *Prélude à l'après-midi d'un faune,* and Bizet *Carmen* Fantasy. Kim and I were both on fire. We played as one organism, and the CD clearly reveals the fever pitch of those performances. At age seventeen, Kim's playing reflected not only the talent and musicianship that won her countless Young Artists' Competitions, but the premature wisdom and insights that I believe were hastened by the many difficult years of our domestic hardships. Thankfully, what is not recorded for posterity is the apt mishap that occurred during our last bows, when her father arose with a quasi-gallant gesture to present us each with a bunch of flowers, tripped on the tape recorder wires, and fell flat on his face. That scene is still stranger than any a fiction writer could have imagined, and I had forgotten it until I heard the concert again.

As I listened, I realized I had undertaken this campaign for myself, as a gift for long years of hard work, and as a proof that Carol Montparker, pianist, was not a figment of my memory, imagination, or vanity. I had a few bizarre fantasies as I sat there on a straight-backed dining room chair, feet up on another chair, impossibly uncomfortable but mesmerized. I wanted to invite every concert pianist I had ever interviewed in my role as music journalist to come over and listen to my CDs. For years I had felt uncomfortably sycophantic as I acted as the catalyst for their egos to flourish, even as I denied my own. Now it would be nice to have their endorsement. On the other hand, I was relieved that I had not had a lifetime of living out of suitcases. André Watts has told me several times that he didn't think "fame" was worth fifty cents. But now I felt clear that it was not fame I coveted—it was recognition. (Just this past year, almost as an uncanny response to these reflections, I was invited by Steinway and Sons to become a part of their distinguished roster of Steinway Artists. That one gesture of recognition was an exciting milestone.)

It is possible and even likely that I will be the main set of ears for my CD collection in years to come, except for the occasional copy I might give to a friend, student, or colleague. I realized after listening that if one were to truly know me, one would have to hear this music.

Mozart, the Starlings,
and My Trigger Finger

E. B. WHITE had his raccoon tree outside his bedroom window, and I have my red-belly tree. The tree and the wildlife it hosted have changed my feelings about the natural world forever, and I learned more than I think I wanted to know.

Two weeks before a chamber music concert, I discovered that a pair of red-bellied woodpeckers, one of my favorite birds, were setting up their domestic life in a pin oak tree right outside our upstairs bedroom window—indeed, only a few feet from our pillows. If we lay very still, Ernest and I could hear the discreet rat-tat-tat as they doggedly hollowed out a dead limb, creating a mound of sawdust on the ground under the tree. Finally they were able to secret themselves inside, and we got to witness their intimate chatterings, their plaintive familial call to each other across the woods, their comings and goings, and, alas, their alarm sounds. Many times as I observed, I identified with White's privileged glimpses of the raccoon life in his tree, and my husband and I made a conscious decision not to share our secret lest we disturb or scare the skittish lovebirds.

Then we spotted the scout on the roof: a lone starling—a rare enough sight, for these birds travel in gangster-mobs, and it didn't bode well; in previous years we had witnessed a pair of flickers and another red-belly pair being violently ousted from their newly bored holes, and we steeled ourselves to experience it again. As we had feared, the band followed, closer and closer, with increasing disregard for the alarm cries and attempts by the woodpeckers and us to scare them away. But we were impotent in the face of the mob of hoodlums. We screamed, rapped on the clapboard of the house, threw stones, and sprayed them with the hose, while they thumbed their beaks at us and at the lovable pair of red-bellies.

Finally the starlings bombarded the hole, and the female, refusing to leave her clutch of eggs, was pecked and mauled mercilessly, crying with the most agonized and pitiable voice I have ever heard from any creature. Time and again she would barely escape the hole, feathers almost in tatters, only to return with the pull of the maternal imperative to get back to her eggs, and to suffer, each time, a gang assault and near murder by the starlings. We heard her muffled cries and whimpers from deep inside the hole and there was not a thing we could do about it. Neither the brave forays and wing-flappings of her mate, nor the appearance of neighborly birds of other species responding to her cries of pain, nor our angry shouts, made any difference to the winged monsters.

At one crazed moment, I yelled from my bedroom window, at the top of my lungs, "Get out, you bastards!" and I chanced to notice some of my next-door neighbors looking up through the thicket of woods that separates our properties, toward my open window. No doubt they thought I had lost my mind and was ousting my dearly beloved husband, as they had no way of knowing about the accursed situation in my oak tree. But my only concern was the increasingly battered state of this poor, intrepid female, whose sad entreaties from nearby perches mingled with the triumphant, shrill whistles of the lowly starlings right outside our window. I didn't think I could ever sleep peacefully there again, and our joy at having the pair was transformed to deep sorrow.

My preoccupation with the tree and its inhabitants subverted my work at the piano. I practiced with one ear cocked for trouble. In my agitation I even cursed my beloved Mozart for having owned a pet starling, not to mention the Shakespearean scholars who brought all those bard-birds, including starlings, to this country, thinking they were doing a good thing. Not the nightingale, nor the chaffinch, nor the bullfinch, nor any of the others survived: only the lowly starling, with no natural enemies here, flourished to the extent that they will inherit our avian realms. On a fateful day in March 1890, one hundred birds were released in New York City's Central Park, and by the 1980s they had increased to over 200 million, according to ornithological studies.

I have tried to love every creature of nature. So I tried to understand why it was that on May 27, 1784, Wolfgang Amadeus Mozart purchased a starling, put it into a cage, and brought it home to listen to its whistles, clicks, rattles, and screeches for inspiration. In fact, caged starlings have been lauded throughout history for their ability to mimic—not only other birds' sounds, but human greetings and conversational fragments as well as household sounds such as doors squeaking and pet sounds. In ancient Greece, Pliny reported that the starlings could mimic Greek and Latin; Shakespeare introduced the starling in his cast of characters in *Henry IV*, and Schubert set to music a poem that describes the bird romantically as having the ability "to speak and sing till every note rang with truth . . . with all the passion of my heart."

Evolution must surely have taken away the starling's voice, perhaps for punishment, because compared with the thrush or any other songbird, its hoarse screams do not qualify as music. (One rarely hears a single starling, as the birds travel in flocks called "murmurations," whereas the thrush is a solitary creature.) I agree with Meredith J. West and Andrew P. King, who, in a scholarly paper, stated that the trouble with starlings was "that they vocalize too much, too often, and in too great numbers, sometimes in cho-ruses numbering in the thousands." Another ornithologist, the late Luis Baptista, with whom I had a friendly correspondence and who had made the study of birdsong a lifetime project, described star-lings as "the vermin of the avian world."

Mozart recorded his purchase of the bird in his expense account along with a transcription of the melody whistled by the bird. He was fascinated and concerned that the starling seemed to whistle a melody similar to a theme from the final movement of his Piano Concerto in G, K. 453, which he was just completing. In fact, that information discouraged me from selecting this particular Mozart concerto for an upcoming engagement. I didn't want to mar a sub-limely beautiful musical experience with any associations with this demonic creature. Mozart was so paranoid about others stealing his music that he sent his manuscript for safekeeping to his father's house in Salzburg. I would gladly assign *any* evil scenario to the bird: perhaps he was sent as a spy (by Salieri?) to steal the melodic material right from under Mozart's nose! It has also been suggested that perhaps Mozart stole the fragment from the starling, but I like the malevolent interpretation much better.

Mozart's *A Musical Joke,* K. 522, has also been linked to his star-ling because of its rambling, amorphous, illogical, and uninspired piecing together of musical fragments, not unlike the ramblings of a starling. Some of the scoring is also deliberately off-key, as a star-ling might sing (if one could call what comes out of such a foul fowl "song"); and the wandering nature of some of the sequences may be said to be reminiscent of the bird's "soliloquies." There are also alternate theories regarding *The Musical Joke,* one of which is that Mozart liked to caricature, in starling style, the music of some of his contemporaries or rivals. But the evidence shows that the composer completed work on K. 522 eight days after the death of the bird, so that it is very likely that the piece is meant as an appropriate sort of requiem for his avian friend. Mozart not only paid tribute to the starling in musical language, he gave it a very decent burial—ironic, considering the great composer's own pauper's funeral. He also immortalized the bird with an ode:

> *A little fool lies here*
> *Whom I held dear*
> *A starling in the prime*
> *Of his brief time*
> *Whose doom it was*
> *To drain Death's bitter pain.*
> *Thinking of this*
> *My heart is riven apart.*
> *O reader, shed a tear,*
> *You also, here.*
> *He was not naughty, quite,*
> *But gay and bright*
> *And under all his brag*
> *A foolish wag.*
> *This no one can gainsay*
> *And I will lay*
> *That he is now on high*
> *And from the sky*
> *Praises me without pay*
> *In his friendly way*
> *Yet unaware that death*
> *Has choked his breath,*
> *And thoughtless of the one*
> *Whose rime is thus well done.*

Well, my sweet Amadeus, whose music raises me higher than any other, let me tell you where your dear starling is, and what he does. Heaven is not at all where he resides, and he is more than a "foolish wag," and much more than "naughty"; and if I can "shed a tear" it is for the havoc he is wreaking around him. His mate is laying her eggs in the nests of lovely songbirds that, as unwitting victims, are hatching those aggressive starling-fledglings alongside their own and losing the battle as the pushier babies get all the food. And they are gaining in biblical proportions while the more fragile species are going extinct.

I tried to obliterate the raucous screams of the robber-birds and the sorrowful laments of the red-bellies outside the window as I worked on the Mozart Piano Concerto in A Major, K. 488, which I chose to prepare for my upcoming concerto engagement. That music reminds me of thrushes and orioles, not starlings.

Down the road a contractor pulled off a logging job to clear a two-acre tract of ancient woods, where he put up nine houses. The more shallow the forestation, the more starlings and the fewer songbirds. I could not practice Mozart with things the way they were, so I decided to go into action.

I went with Ernest to a sporting-equipment store and bought a BB gun, much to Ernest's and my own shock and dismay. The two of us, activists against the National Rifle Association, in the gun department! This fifteen-dollar firearm is not illegal and will not kill; but it will scare away the starlings, or so we thought. I came home and took a position on my bed pillow by the open window, with the BB gun aimed at the contested hole like a veritable sniper. Thus transformed into a pistol-packin' pianist, I pinged each and every starling that showed up until they got the point and the red-bellies could return. The female red-belly entered the hole and began dumping out the starlings' debris and twigs that had littered her laboriously excavated limb. Bit by bit, string and twigs and indistinguishable flotsam and jetsam tumbled out while we kept guard, feeling secretly hopeful. The moment we turned our backs, however, it happened again. Her tortured shrieks told us the gangsters had returned. Somehow they had the uncanny instinct of divining when she had been left unprotected.

By now I began to realize that I had developed a terrible tendonitis in my "trigger finger" (formerly known as my second finger), along with a fierce muscle spasm in my neck, from my twisted position as I lay poised for action at the window. Considering the way my body was protesting, I was getting a bit anxious about my concert the following day of a Beethoven quintet and a Bach sonata.

I posed the question to myself: *What do you care more about, the concert or the woodpeckers?* The answer came up: *The woodpeckers.* I cannot account for my priorities; but it was clear that nature, formerly my muse, was becoming an adversary, about to wreck my concert! Eventually, after a few more assays, Ernest and I had to accept the harsh reality: there was no fighting Mother Nature—the starlings would win this and any other fray. The same scenario is going on in my friend Lillie's yard, and no doubt in everyone else's.

I went to the piano, uninspired, and tried to get back to the music; it took a long time to get my juices flowing again, and I could hardly concentrate for the cries of the little victims. When I left the piano to water the garden, a blue jay darted out from the ilex hedge inches from the spigot for the hose. A closer look revealed her tightly woven nest with its three speckled eggs. I won't even contemplate what would have happened to my hand if I had tried to turn the hose on once the eggs were hatched, but at least this batch I would be able to protect from the starlings and cowbirds who try to lay on top of the jay's brood. I would simply reach in and throw the parasitic clutch out. (My life here in paradise is clearly destined to be a struggle for me and my birds.)

The concert went terrifically well, and a few weeks later, while gardening in light rain, I realized that the airwaves were free of the starlings' grackling and wheezing, and I was hearing only the birdsongs of species I loved—cardinals, orioles, titmice, chickadees, goldfinches, and so on; the starlings seemed to have vacated the nest (having released yet more of their undesirable progeny into the skies). As though they had been on hold, the pair of red-bellies suddenly appeared to reclaim their hole. For several hours, I enjoyed their animated interactions and watched the streamers of debris float down from the hole as they yet again set to cleaning house. It had been raining for three straight days and everything was soaked. Later in the day a lone starling appeared and started harassing them, and the bickering turned more inflamed; but now the woodpeckers seemed more aggressive, defending the limb with a vengeance. I stayed out of it, but by evening it seemed that the female woodpecker was ensconced in the hole.

Around ten o'clock that night, we were in bed when we heard a struggle and then a crash. Dreading the worst, I resisted leaping out of bed, and somehow fell asleep hoping that a burglar had broken into the porch, rather than the more horrible scenario.

At six in the morning, I heard both the woodpecker's plaintive cry and the starling's shrieks. I looked out of the window and saw the male red-bellied woodpecker perched on the jagged edges of what was left of that fateful limb, which had apparently broken off. A glance down at the ground revealed chunks and flakes of wood. I put on my robe and slippers and hurried downstairs and outside. There on the ground was the major portion of the bough, which had broken off exactly in the middle of the freshly engorged nesting hole. The dead limb, drenched by rain and stressed by the weight and wear of two warring species, gave way and dropped, leaving the lower half of the dugout open to the sky. The woodpecker was trying to sit and cover whatever was left of their clutch of eggs, and several more starlings had also returned to the scene.

My husband and I sadly brought the chunk of dead wood (which not only had half this season's fresh cavity, but an old hole from seasons past) onto the porch as a kind of memorial totem to the valiant red-bellies, and as a monolithic shrine at which to pray for the future of all endangered species.

The Blue Piano

DURING the exciting months following the publication of my book *A Pianist's Landscape,* I gave talks and lecture-recitals all over the place, and no one gave me a better party than the Steinway company. The event, in celebration of the book, was to be held in the elegant rotunda of their landmark building on 57th Street, one of the most beautiful spaces in New York City. The lamp-lit salon, with its marble arches and columns and domed ceiling, is decorated with a Waterford crystal chandelier, luxurious furniture, and beautiful paintings. The walls are lined with portraits of the many illustrious artists whose names are historically linked with Steinway, including Sergei Rachmaninoff, Anton Rubinstein, Arthur Rubinstein, and Vladimir Horowitz. A florid depiction of "Beethoven in Nature" by N. C. Wyeth hangs with paintings by Harry Townsend of Handel, Wagner, and Mozart (on his deathbed, surrounded by musicians). All along the polished wood hallways are signed photographs of every pianist who ever graced the site.

The salon is a stylish and fanciful place, with its floor-to-ceiling windows right on the street for passers-by to look into, or for guests to look out at the pedestrians and traffic on one of the city's most sophisticated thoroughfares.

When the evening drew near, my fantasies of the event to be

held in my honor ran from the guest list to what dress I would wear and mundane details such as the champagne and desserts. One of the last details I thought about was the piano itself. I remembered several occasions on which I was invited to choose a piano from the Steinway basement, a veritable sea of black whales; they could have given me almost any of those pianos and I would have been quite happy. It was the densest population of fine instruments anywhere, and so that was my least concern.

It was only an afterthought that prompted me to call early on the day of the Steinway celebration to check about last-minute arrangements and to ask the hostess in charge, Patricia Prudente, "What kind of piano will I have for the concert?" I must have been wondering about the size, more than anything else: would it be a nine-foot concert Model D or a seven-foot Model B?

"Oh, you are so lucky," she replied, with great enthusiasm. "You will be playing the Gershwin Centennial Piano!"

"What is that?" I asked, with only the first faint twinge of dread.

"Oh, we have only issued twenty-four of these wonderful instruments, in honor of the one hundredth birthday of George Gershwin."

"Yes, but what are they like?" I insisted.

"Well, the piano is royal blue," she began.

My hair stood on end, whilst down the drain went any images of elegance I had conjured up for the recital.

She continued: "It's an Art Deco design, the music desk is carved like the skyline of Manhattan, and the word 'Rhapsody' is in gilt lettering with gold stars on the case."

I heard myself murmur, "I don't play blue pianos. . . . " My voice trailed off. But pretty soon I recovered myself and my breath to declare emphatically and passionately, "I cannot play such a piano tonight. I am playing Schubert, Mozart, Chopin, Bach—there must be at least a hundred thousand fine black pianos in this building. Surely you can get a *normal* black piano for me to play?"

"Carol, this is the piano that has been placed in the salon for your concert tonight," she explained patiently. "It has been featured in the window all week in celebration of Gershwin's birthday, and we cannot take it out of the salon. It has already been tuned for you. You should feel fortunate to play a special instrument like this one. It's really a remarkably beautiful piano, with a great tone," she scolded.

"Let me explain myself," I ventured. "I am a very visual person. I am *used* to black pianos. It will most certainly throw me off to sit down at a royal blue piano and try to make serious music. May I call the manager of the house?"

"No," she stated firmly. "I will call you back, but I doubt there is time to remove this instrument and move and tune up another. But I will do my best."

I added one last remark. "Let's put it this way: it really will make or break my evening. In fact, I have to tell you, I am so disappointed that I already have lost any sense of happy anticipation of this evening's event."

Indeed, sitting down at a Disney-like cartoon of a piano, as I envisioned it, instead of the shiny black concert grands that we are so accustomed to playing, would have been a nightmare for me. I had entirely lost my sense of humor; the mere thought of it, and the terrible waiting period I had to suffer, caused me to do what I usually do in crises: eat some chocolate and go out shopping, in this case for a pair of beautiful earrings. When I returned, there was a happy message on my machine: Patricia had succeeded in procuring me a lovely *black* Model D piano that would be tuned and ready for the recital by the time I arrived. As relieved and grateful as I was, I couldn't help thinking what might have happened had I never asked and simply arrived that evening expecting to see a gorgeous black concert grand waiting for me in the elegant salon and finding that gaudy blue impostor instead.

I have encountered my share of PSOs ("piano-shaped-objects") on stages where I was about to play. Those babies *look* as though they might sound fine, but that's where the resemblance ends. In this case, though, the instrument probably *sounded* beautiful, but it looked so outrageous that I could not go near it. I did approach it after the party, where my friend, the pianist Jerry Lowenthal, and I discovered it standing in one of the smaller salons in Steinway Hall. Jerry lost not a second before sitting right down at the improbable keyboard, gleefully lacing into the one and only piece that suited the piano perfectly: Gershwin's *Rhapsody in Blue*.

The Gershwin centennial piano was one in a stream of special "art cases" that have been a colorful part of Steinway's history. Many of them are pictured in a big coffee-table book called *Steinway* and are designated "fancy pianos." I can picture myself giving a concert of Couperin, Rameau, and even Mozart, on the ornate Vanderbilt Steinway, commissioned in 1893 and decorated in Paris with pale green and gilt carving and panels of rococo paintings reminiscent of Watteau and Boucher. The first of two White House pianos is quite beautiful too, with its painting under the lid of the nine muses: Clio (history), Calliope (epic poetry), Melpomene (tragedy), Euterpe (music), Polyhymnia (religious music), Thalia (comedy), Terpsichore (dance), Urania (astronomy), and Erato (lyric poetry.) The design of that piano was directed by Joseph Burr Tiffany, and it was presented to Theodore Roosevelt in 1903. I could play anything on that instrument, certainly with the strong support of all those muses. But on the second White House piano, given during Franklin Delano Roosevelt's term of office in 1938, with its gold eagles supporting the body of the instrument, and folk-music motifs in gold all around the mahogany case, I fear I could only play Sousa, Gottschalk, and Stephen Foster.

I shared the tale of the blue piano with many of my sympathetic pianist-friends. When I asked André Watts several weeks later whether he thought I had acted like a prima donna by refusing to play the Gershwin Centennial Piano, he exclaimed, "Absolutely not! I would never play a blue piano either!" adding, "Do you mean now when we check ahead about the piano we get on tour, we not only have to ask about the condition, but the color too?"

Claude Frank, who helped me with the scheduling of my subsequent book talk and recital at the Yale School of Music where he teaches, was clearly amused by the story. I arrived at the school the evening of my lecture-recital, and as I entered the lobby of the music building, I was handed a note in Claude's handwriting: "Hi Carol. Go right on up to the hall, and I will meet you there soon. The piano is waiting for you. By the way, it is *black!*"

Suffering Indignities

THE steam radiator shrieked its high A-flats through the sleep-less night as I lay in bed in the musty Victorian inn, wonder-ing whether it had been worth driving up to this small New England college town to play. A train wailed its diminished sev-enth chord through a nearby crossing. It was a harmless little conceit and distraction, identifying the pitches of odd sounds—bird calls, trucks' brakes, squeaky hinges, car alarms—a condi-tioned reflex and a game with relatively little value as an element of musicianship. But this night in bed, my game was scant rec-ompense for the situation I had had to deal with earlier that day.

Every now and then the geographic boundaries of my smallish musical sphere have seemed stifling, even though they have been self-imposed so that I could have a fairly normal domestic life out-side of the piano. The rationale that audiences are the same all over has, most of the time, been enough to keep me content without traveling far. I have passed up many opportunities to play out of town; I love my home, and I do not like the hassle of traveling. But sometimes an invitation comes along that sounds enticing.

When the chairman of the piano department of a large uni-versity invited me to play in Amherst, a town sprinkled with col-leges, I was so eager to meet and play for the music students from the surrounding campuses that the 250-mile drive seemed effortless. The gig came in the middle of a book tour that brought me from New York City up to Yale in Connecticut, so it was on the trajectory. I used the driving time to reflect and refine the lecture-recital format in my head. The professor had suggested the grand old library in the center of town as a focal point that would attract students from all the colleges in the town, and cited the fact that there was a good Steinway piano there.

"I came to try the piano. I'm giving a concert here tonight," I told the director of the beautiful library.

"The key to the Meeting Room is at the circulation desk. Leave your license or credit card with the clerk," she answered in a monotone, while her eyes stayed glued to the papers she was shuffling on her desk.

Affronted by her rudeness, I did as I was bade, and finally encountered the conspicuously ancient Steinway grand, thick with dust, wedged into a corner, up against a radiator—all of which did not bode well. The instrument was hemmed in by audio-visual equipment, and there was no piano bench in sight. I returned to the forbidding director.

"I cannot budge the piano away from the wall and there are no seats set up for this evening's event. Is there a custodian to help me?"

"Your concert was arranged by a university professor. We do not make the library's staff and services available to other organizations." These words were uttered in the style of a concentration camp matron, and I could hardly believe that these were the conditions under which I was expected to make music.

An hour earlier, I had cased the joint looking for any visible sign that my concert existed. I had sent batches of flyers to the library, to the various music departments of each college and university in the town, and to a former student living in the town who attended one of the colleges, with a letter of request that the flyers be posted on bulletin boards or distributed to students. One of the realities of choosing a career with a small c, on one's own terms and at one's own rhythms, is that one is printer, publicist, and PR person, as well as pianist. I don't mind that, but coming to a town where there doesn't seem to be one small shred of publicity anywhere in sight, is a blow, to be sure.

I called the chairman of the music department who had invited me to tell her how un-thrilled I was about the status of things, and she was horrified, although I think I was more horrified than she. I went back down to the basement hall in the library and began shoving things around. Somehow I got the equipment off the piano, removed the dusty canvas cover, wheeled the big old brown baby to the middle of the room, and put some rows of chairs into a semicircle. Finally, with whatever wind I had left inside of me, I tried the piano. It was hopelessly out of tune, and when I had the nerve to ask the matron/director of the library whether it could be tuned, I got the response I expected in the tone I anticipated.

I stood there taking stock of the realities: I had to play the program at eight o'clock that evening on an out-of-tune piano flimsy with age, albeit with traces of its once pretty tone (which is what the professor who had recommended this hall had remembered), and hopefully someone would show up to hear it. In fact, eight people did. One of them was an unfortunate man, who looked as though he might be homeless and who approached me clutching some music manuscript paper as I was preparing to begin my program. He asked me whether I would play the music that he had composed.

"No, I am sorry, but I have already chosen my program. But I wish you good luck with your manuscript."

He left. Now seven people sat waiting for me to begin, including the unhappy (though not as unhappy as I), totally sympathetic piano professor.

I made up my mind to give the handful of folks the full treatment, rather than a watered-down version of my program that would be proportional to the number sitting there. Casting aside the disappointments, I threw myself into the lecture-recital with the same force of love, energy, and devotion I always feel during performances, whatever the circumstances. After I finished, those seven applauded as though they were a multitude. The professor stood up and put her hand up to stop the applause so she could speak to the few listeners. I must admit I felt a momentary twinge of regret that she was cutting short my hard-earned reward, until I heard what she said:

"I want to . . . no, I *have* to say something. Sometimes you go to a concert and you hear a fine musician on a beautiful instrument and you enjoy the concert. But when you hear a fine musician on a neglected piano, and under these adverse conditions, and she *still* manages to make beautiful music, then it is particularly moving and extraordinary. What we have witnessed tonight was a rare privilege." And then the seven broke out into more applause. I felt strangely gratified and satisfied that there was, after all, a good reason I drove up to the town.

Rock stars fill football stadiums and classical musicians can hardly fill a community library. The recital series I used to run in our own village library attracted excellent musicians because of the fine Steinway, good acoustics, and decent honoraria. In spite of adequate publicity, there were times I had to accost the few people (five to ten at most) sitting and waiting for the artist to appear and solicit quarters from them so I could stand in the lobby at the pay phone and commandeer anyone I found at home to hop in the car and attend the concert; I did not want the artist to be demoralized by facing a near-empty room. (Is the public at large ungrateful? Do they tend to reject whatever they can get for nothing?) Sometimes the library director invited nursing home patients to fill the seats; yes, there were bodies filling the seats, but soon the snoring, talking, and fidgeting canceled out any benefits.

An invitation to play in a private home sometimes reveals another kind of insensitivity. Many years ago, my son and I were hired to give a benefit cello and piano concert in someone's home. After we arrived, we were ushered into the bedroom and told, " Wait until we summon you." It reminded me of the famous story of the world-famous violinist hired to play at the mansion of a very wealthy hostess, who asked him his fee.

"Ten thousand dollars," he replied.

"You understand, you are not to mingle with my guests," she instructed.

"In that case," responded the violinist, spokesperson for all suffering artists, "my fee is only five thousand dollars."

Before a benefit concert for a large scientific institution, I arrived a half-hour early. Needing a quiet room to collect my thoughts before going onto the stage, I asked the woman in charge where I could sit by myself.

"What are you so nervous about, dearie?" she asked in a snippy voice.

Without replying, I wandered away and entered an empty office, sat down, and tried to think about the music, when suddenly she appeared out of nowhere and said,

"Oh no! You cannot stay in here! This is *my* office!"

I meandered around in search of a broom closet in which to install myself, but by then it was time to begin.

A week before the main event of the season, the director of an arts organization was promised a lulu of an interview from a major newspaper. She rounded up the soloists, and we came from all directions, giving up an afternoon of work to gather for the photo opportunity. It was clear from the first moments of the meeting that the journalist from this prestigious publication had a good case of pomposity and self-importance.

She asked a few questions of the director and then, without any warning, snapped, "Will you allow me to speak to the artists themselves, please?" as though the director would have any objection at all.

Having got her number, we handled her gingerly, fielding her questions with great caution and not without a bit of false deference. Our eyes were darting around, and many a giggle was stifled. Then the photographer, who was from the same esteemed establishment, walked in and asked us to "pretend he wasn't there" and to "do what we do." We walked over to the piano and posed ourselves around the instrument.

"Oh no, no, no!" said the photographer. "We do not take posed pictures."

"Oh, this *is* what we do!" exclaimed the foxy artistic director. "We gather around the piano and discuss the score!" Whereupon we all feigned earnest scrutiny of some music which had nothing whatever to do with our upcoming concert.

I pointed to one phrase and said to the oboist (with whom I had no collaboration), "We should play this passage *pianissimo.*"

Almost losing his composure, he answered me, with equal mock seriousness, "Perhaps a *subito piano.*"

Then everyone else got into the act, pointing to random, meaningless spots on the printed page, making nonsensical and hilarious (to us) "musical" decisions while secretly mocking the journalist, who was clearly a charlatan in the field of the arts and looked impressed at our profound artistic interaction. Meanwhile the photographer, convinced that he was catching candid and penetrating shots of the creative process, snapped off quite a number of random combinations from the group.

The director and the soloists were a bit concerned that none of the shots seemed to include all of us together: some of us would make it into the paper, and others would not, it seemed, in spite of the fact that we had all, in the interests of publicity, sacrificed our time to be there. The director courageously decided to suggest that the photographer back up and try to get us all in; the journalist and photographer ignored her.

The biggest affront came when the photographer asked the director to place her violin upon the piano so he could get a "still life" of the two instruments and some sheet music.

"Surely you aren't thinking of using a photo of two inanimate objects for the article, when all these artists gave up their day to come here for the photograph!"

The reporter rose, puffed herself up, and bellowed, "You *may* be the director of an arts organization, but you are *not* the director of our newspaper. Do not tell us how to do our business!" The photographer, who seemed to be suffering from the same delusions of grandeur as the reporter, echoed her sentiments. There was a deafening silence in the auditorium, and our artistic director walked out of the hall, leaving us alone with the two stiffs from the newspaper. We answered some last questions with minimal engagement. Within a short time, both arrogant individuals left to try to belittle some other fools who thought they were lucky to be interviewed by the renowned newspaper, and we each returned to our normal lives.

I have conducted many an interview for numerous publications, always with a sense of appreciation for the time and energy artists give over in return for the chance to gain some recognition for their hard work. In this case, the journalist and the photographer acted as though they had done *us* a big favor in coming. In the end, we got the payoff we could have expected: the promised article never appeared in the paper.

It feels so much better once it's all a matter of record.

Brooklyn

I'M a Brooklyn girl, and to paraphrase someone's sagacious words, "You can take the girl out of Brooklyn, but you can't take Brooklyn out of the girl." I am chauvinistic and nostalgic about the New York borough, and it is possible that traces of the regional dialect faintly tinge my speech. I can discern that verbal imprint, however obscure, in anyone else, but I remain blithely innocent—or in denial—of its presence in my own speech.

Each time I drive over the Verrazano Narrows Bridge, along Gravesend Bay in Brooklyn, images, sounds, and smells from my early childhood bubble up to the surface. My family bicycled there along the water, and one can walk to the street where we lived from the shore. My parents rented the second floor of an old frame house with a wraparound porch; perhaps it was a bit dilapidated, as my mother frequently lamented, but I believe that in those eleven formative years I spent there, until we moved to Long Island, the character and charm of the place left deep and indelible traces that I could later link to preferences in my adult life.

I will teach my grandchildren the childhood games I played around that house. A slab of concrete in the backyard was one focal point: upon it we drew a potsy court, and played hopscotch and ball games, bouncing the Spalding India rubber ball and chanting "A my name is Alice and my husband's name is Al, we come from Alabama and we sell apples, B . . . " until the ball hit a crack and we were out. We played hit the penny and threw the ball in the air, clapping as many times as we could before catching it. In the street we played ring-a-levio, a higher form of hide-and-seek, and line soccer. On our cement front steps we played "stoopball." "Stoop" is one of my favorite words. It sounds Brooklynese, although I am certain they have stoops in other towns; but a Brooklyn stoop, or better, a Brooklyn street lined with stoops, is a picturesque and evocative image to me, because of the leisure hours spent there, not only by kids but by their families as well. The nondescript foliage and grasses from around the property, and in the empty lot next door, became the foodstuffs for our imaginary fruit and vegetable markets. (In those days we could play in empty, overgrown lots without fear.) We never had a Toys "R" Us, and we never needed one.

There were inviting trees that drooped umbrellalike fronds, creating secret hideaways under which I could wheel my doll carriage, spread a blanket, and read my favorite books, mostly by Louisa May Alcott. I can remember the shrubs and trees so vividly that now, years later, I can put the proper botanical names to them: bearded iris, lilacs, hydrangeas, mock orange, and hollyhocks.

My tiny bedroom, which might have been a cubicle to anyone else, was my haven, looking out into a huge cherry tree with clouds of white blossoms that later yielded the delicious yellow cherries, each with a blush of rosy red, that we could pick right from the fire escape. I remember an outdoor birthday party for my sister, one June, under that blossoming tree.

Childhood dwellings can be the source of both joys and fears with long-ranging effects. One of the ongoing joys in my life, which is to have my bed beside a window where I can see the sky, look up into the branches of a tree, and feel the breezes across me as I sleep, came from the childhood classic *Heidi,* by Johanna Spyri, which I read in Brooklyn. Heidi's little bed of straw in the loft of her grandfather's barn seemed to me to be the most exquisite pleasure a child could have. And so I had my parents move my bed to the window. But I can trace one of my phobias to that window as well. One dark night, I was startled to see an otherworldly phantom with dazzling lights: an enormous zeppelin, illuminated by blinking advertisements, looming low, that led me to harbor a residual, lifelong dread of blimps. My other phobia is spiders, which I can trace to the enormous specimen of a tree spider that made itself right at home in its sparkling new iridescent web on top of the privet hedge in front of our stoop. It appeared suddenly after a dangerous hurricane felled one of the great maples that lined our street. The creature was riveting, especially through the exaggerated lens of a child's eye—the size of an open hand, decorated with every color of the rainbow—and we had to pass right by it each time we left the house. That image embodied "the fascination of the abomination" for me.

But those monumental maples also yielded pleasures. I loved the smell of chlorophyll that they gave off in early spring, and I loved the spicy autumn aromas that accompanied our shuffling steps through the mounds of crunchy fallen leaves. The "pugnoses" (which is what we called the seedpods that fell, twirling like tiny helicopters) we stuck across the bridges of our noses.

These were the war years. My father was a welder in the Brooklyn Navy Yard and had some near-death experiences when he stepped on live electrical wires as he worked, knee-deep in water. At night he was an air-raid warden, and the sound of those wailing sirens, along with the closing of shades and curtains during blackouts, were our personal scary war experiences. Those days are etched in my mind as proof of his invincibility, more deeply embossed by my entreaties to him, through subsequent years, to relate

the adventures of what we began to call his "nine lives." Our favorite tale was his fabled cross-country trip on the tops of freight
trains in his early youth during the depression. The image of my father as a handsome young man, hiding from railroad guards alongside of hoboes, freezing at night and baking in the desert sun atop
those freight cars, just to get to Hollywood and try to make it, was
a folly that deeply endeared him to me. There were motorcycle accidents, falls from fire escapes, and near-drownings. Now past
ninety and still climbing up on a ladder to clean his gutters, he has
more than surpassed nine lives.

My mother has had her fascinating tales to tell as well, including
what she knows of her mother's ancestors, scholars from Lithuania,
who walked across the Caucasus to get to the Promised Land. My
grandmother (whom I never knew) was born in Palestine (way before the establishment of the State of Israel). Her first husband had
been killed by an Arab while working as a manager in the vineyards
belonging to the Baron de Rothschild. As a result of that tragedy,
my grandmother, under the protection and sponsorship of the Rothschild family, left Palestine and went to Paris with her young
daughter, only to suffer the death of that baby from typhus. Ultimately, she resettled in the United States and met my grandfather,
a pharmacist, who died when my mother was only three.

As a young girl, my mother went with her mother to visit Palestine, and she revisited the region later as a young woman. I cherish
the tales she told to my sister and me about living and working in
the Mediterranean, including her job with the one of the directors
of the English-run Iraq Petroleum Company, which was laying an
oil pipeline across the desert to the sea. Her stories are even more
spellbinding to me now, especially the notion that a young Jewish
woman lived without serious consequence in an Arab-dominated,
historically combustible region for those few years.

Little remnants of my mother's Middle Eastern experiences

vividly dotted my childhood Brooklyn home: artifacts like the lovely chartreuse-colored "vase" (which was really part of a Turkish hookah), a burnished brass platter embossed with a scene from the Old Testament depicting King Solomon, a wooden camel's seat, and a few choice Arabic maledictions she could utter if the situation warranted it. I am always struck by the irony my mother frequently underscored regarding the countless similarities between the Hebrew and Arabic languages and culture, especially the words for peace, *shalom* and *salaam*.

I recall my mother's ever feisty and resourceful role during the war years of economic struggle in the Brooklyn of my childhood. She would sometimes step into the middle of the road, bucket in hand, to stop a coal truck, thus eking out fuel to get us through yet a few more winter nights. She was (and still is) so pretty that usually the driver even came around the back of the house, carrying the pail of coal to the outdoor trapdoors that flapped open to the chutes to the furnace.

In the spring, right alongside those slanted trapdoors, we planted our victory garden, rows and rows of vegetables designated by neat little empty packets on stakes to identify the various seedlings as they emerged from the soil. Perhaps it was then I also sowed the seeds of my lifelong love of gardening.

One day in April 1944, I found my mother and our downstairs neighbor crying in the hallway; they had just learned of FDR's death. But then, in the tangle of early childhood recollections, it seems that not so long afterward (it was actually, of course, August 1945), there were block parties celebrating the end of the war, and we were allowed to stay up all night and walk the few blocks in the dark to our cousins Howard, Nora, Stuart, and Arthur's block parties. Folks had placed long tables in the middle of their streets and brought offerings from their homes: casseroles, salads, desserts, a veritable feast after all those years of austerity. In bright daylight hours we threaded red, white, and blue crepe-paper streamers in and out of the spokes of our bicycles, while parades of returning troops, soldiers, sailors, marines, and tanks marched triumphantly down Bay Parkway, just half a block from our house.

It was in that old house that my mother taught me the rudiments of music after I showed an early aptitude for it on my grandfather's upright at age three. Then, despite some raised eyebrows from friends and family, my parents sacrificed to buy me my first piano, even with their strapped financial circumstances. It was a baby grand with the name Settegren on it, a name I have never heard of since, and it usurped the major portion of our tiny living room; I vividly remember the day it was moved in. Shortly thereafter Mother found me my first "real" piano teacher, Miss Esther R. Bernstein, a few blocks away. Thus was I launched into a study that was to become my profession.

Half a block away was my public school, P.S. 128, with its darkly paneled hallways and the awe-inspiring auditorium in which I had my first public appearances. We were required to wear white middy blouses, dark blue skirts, and red ties to the weekly assembly programs, and the smell of clean white cotton being ironed by my mother on assembly days is still evoked for me each time I press clean linen.

Brooklyn is sometimes reduced to a kaleidoscopic collage of image fragments and vignettes: my father running alongside me as I learned to ride my bike; my big, amply bosomed, cozy paternal grandmother coming down the street brandishing a jumbo-sized Hershey bar for me (the probable origin of my lifelong downfall!); our small kitchen, traces of which I so often have seen in antique flea markets: the metal-top extension table with its leaves that pulled and snapped out, the charred old stovetop grill and cover in which my mother placed a piece of brown paper and baked potatoes, chicken livers, and the delectable unborn eggs that were sometimes found inside the chicken. At that table one day, I took my mother aback with the million-dollar question "Mommy, what are the facts of life?" after classmates had challenged me, in a singsong voice, to prove to them that I knew. I knew nothing. As I remember, her response was an artful combination of just enough science, laced with lots of euphemism and the assurance "You will know what to do when the time comes," to satisfy a curious ten-year-old.

Sometimes we walked to 86th Street to the Benson theater, which had matinees of double features plus cartoons and fat matrons bossing the unruly kids back into their seats. After the show we got charlottes russes—darling, delectable little now-extinct round cakes topped with whipped cream, chocolate sprinkles, and a cherry. Above the stores was the elevated BMT (Brooklyn-Manhattan Transit) line, where the trains screeched and threw sparks down through the rails and supports to the street; this was the very station from which I had to force myself, in spite of motion sickness, to take a weekly subway ride to my lessons in New York City, once Miss Bernstein insisted, when I was eight, that I study with her teacher, Mr. Harold Henry.

He was a formidable bachelor type who lived in an elegant 57th Street apartment building with his two Welsh corgies, enormous, intricately carved Chinese furniture, rugs upon rugs, and ornate oversized ginger jars, all of which put me into a state of awe as I waited in his foyer for my lesson. Then I was confronted with his glass eye and his monocled good eye. In spite of all those exotic distractions, I probably even learned a few things from him about the piano in those two years; recently I discovered his name in Harold C. Schonberg's book *The Great Pianists*. Somewhere I have his black-and-white photo, which he presented to me with a flourish, inscribed, "To Carol, whose talent will take her far, if she is industrious and careful."

Soon afterward we moved to Forest Hills, primarily to be nearer to Leopold Mittman, whom my mother had read about and intuitively felt to be the right teacher for me. He was not only the right one, he became the single most important influence in my life. I left behind my Brooklyn friends whose Jewish and Italian names have seemed to be mysteriously reduced to musical sounds: Bernicelefkowitz, Cynthiadangelo, Donnakatz, Robertmatucci, and Loiswexler, the little showoff.

My husband and I attended a Bargemusic recital on a barge permanently moored in the East River, right in the shadow of the Brooklyn Bridge, that has been converted into a small concert hall. I couldn't help feeling that I might want to play a concert there one day in celebration of my beloved Brooklyn. I would have to overcome the slight seasickness caused by the rocking of the boat in the wake of all the river traffic, and the sense of being upstaged by the brilliant backdrop of gulls flying past the enormous glass window revealing the entire Manhattan skyline, not to mention all manner of watercraft sailing by.

On the way home from that concert, we purposely took the Belt Parkway so that I could make a detour to revisit my old frame house on 83rd Street, in Bensonhurst. As the car approached, my heart was pounding with excitement and curiosity. Slowly we proceeded east from 21st Avenue, perusing the left side of the street with its odd-numbered dwellings, and then, to my horror, came a hideous row of attached houses with plastic shingle siding; evidently they had torn down our picturesque old wooden house and put up this ugly row.

I thought, *It's a mistake to look back. The past is basically dead. I should have stopped short of disturbing my gentle memories.*

Just months after my disappointing trip back to my childhood block, an exciting event that none of us could ever have foretold reestablished my family's link to Brooklyn in an even deeper sense: my cousin Stuart Mont and his wife, Annette, rescued and restored an historic Dutch farmhouse there. The last surviving member of a family with lineage dating from early settlers had died and left no heirs. A second husband wanted no part of the property and priced it to sell immediately. My cousins heard that the beautiful old house, on an acre of land amidst apartment buildings, was going to be sold to developers, who would raze it to put up more tall buildings. Stu and Annette were able to purchase the house for a song, because the plumbing, heating, and all the facilities were antiquated and any updating would have to be done within the strictures of the tightly monitored National Landmark Association. But my cousins are adventuresome and Stu is very handy, so they bought the house and plunged into the modernization project without disturbing a shred of the atmosphere.

When they took title, they expected to find a bare house, and were flabbergasted to find that the price that they had paid also included all the contents, which were probably worth more than the house itself. There were marvelous antiques including enormous seventeenth-century Dutch cupboards, numerous sets of old china and silverware, cookware, kitchen implements, an entire houseful of quite valuable furnishings, rugs, and even a piano. My own favorite facet of their bonanza was discovered in the attic and in an antique chifforobe: a cache of at least fifteen gorgeous handmade quilts, some so precious that they were even signed by the Dutch settler women who stitched them. Stu loves to bring them out of their careful storage to exhibit one by one to lucky visitors. In the barn are sleighs, harnesses, and a bounty of books, many in their first editions, along with stacks of music flaking into oblivion. In the basement is a printing press not unlike the one Benjamin Franklin used, with trays of type, shelves of ink, cards, and all the accoutrements of a print shop. The press especially moved Ernest, who was born in another part of Brooklyn; when he was an infant, his crib had been placed adjacent to his father's old printing press. Outside in the yard are traces of old perennial gardens and an arbor that still bears vines and abundant bunches of grapes, which we tasted. I am forgetting many of the astounding details shown to us the day we had a family reunion in their house, when the restoration was complete.

Annette gave me an antique straw bonnet from the house, in perfectly good shape, which I often don as I garden, with a strong sense of my colonial counterpart in her Brooklyn garden.

I find it most amazing to come upon this acre clearing and view a sight straight out of the 1700s, especially the notion that members of my own family live there. The terms of the deed stipulated that my cousins act as stewards of the estate and allow certain hours for visitors. Stu and Annette have occupied the premises for a number of years and made memorable contributions to its restoration. It is not beyond possibility that they will some day find it appropriate and not disrespectful to add our last name to the plaque at the gate, designating the landmark "The Ryder-Bennett-*Mont* Homestead." (Wouldn't my grandparents, who came from Eastern Europe near the beginning of the twentieth century, be proud?)

The Best Journal

FROM the time my father began to photograph my sister and me as young children wearing self-conscious smirks and my mother looking impatient, through my first marriage to a compulsive shutterbug for whom no experience was complete unless it was recorded on film, I have had an antipathy for cameras. Now both my husband and I find it burdensome when we travel, and we have developed a deeply satisfying alternate way of recording our journeys.

We keep journals. Mine are filled with quick watercolor sketches done on the spot with corresponding chronicling of my thoughts, and my husband's are loggings of each day, sparked with poetry—which is to say his paintings in words.

For our honeymoon in England and Scotland, we bought ourselves matching clothbound books with spanking white pages that we knew we could not resist filling. I purchased a tiny Winsor and Newton travel watercolor set with highly concentrated pigments requiring just a bit of water, and one fine versatile brush with several felt-tip pens for sketching and writing.

In the airport lounge when our flight was delayed several hours, Ernest wrote his reflections of our wedding party while I sketched travelers in varying degrees of impatience and anxiety.

146

It completely assuaged my own. Once we got to our hotel in London, upon being told our room would not be ready for another hour, I sketched the elegant lobby while Ernest had tea and jotted down his passing thoughts. The next day we arrived early for the theater, and the manager let us into the empty hall so I could sketch. Street scenes, pubs, bobbies, double-decker buses, timbered old houses, and a Thames boat ride to Hampton Court were all gaily depicted as I began to fill my pages with color. A teenaged girl who looked like a walking piece of graffiti, with hot-pink spiked hair and a punk get-up, was positively thrilled when I told her that I wanted to sketch her creative costume.

Another day at Victoria Station I did a pretty good painting while waiting for our train to come in of the huge erector-set-like vaulted structure over the tracks. By rail we passed through bright yellow and green pastures, craggy patches of gorse, and Roman aqueducts alongside the North Sea, and up into Scotland. I did fast impressions of the landscape from the moving train to test my visual acuity.

Every evening Ernest and I had our little ritual of trading journals to share our personal reflections, each sometimes surprising the other with an unexpected point of view. In Edinburgh, a secret garden outside our bedroom window at the Arden Hotel caught my fancy, and I jotted down the notes of an unfamiliar birdsong. When I review those pages I can hear the nightingales, whose trills we heard from our bed that was made up with freshly sun-dried linens. A photo could never bring all that back to me.

In the Lake District I painted the shaggy mountain goats after we scooted them off the "bonnet" of our rented car in Elterwater. On the page across from my sketch of Wordsworth's Dove Cottage in Grasmere, I copied the poet's vision of the place. Then I ventured some lines of my own. But it is Ernest's book that holds some truly beautiful poems. One of my journal pages is titled

"Ernest the poet, Ullswater, June 8." He was writing at the moment I was sketching him.

The next day I painted a profusion of wildflowers annotated with their Latin names. No photo, I daresay, would recapture their fragility and vividness for me as did the illustration I was lucky to put down on that page. And as I painted, Ernest wrote in his journal (which I read later that evening), "She is like these wildflowers—sudden, delicate, richly-colored, with surprising, wonderful beauty." That moment was frozen in time by our journals, although he still sometimes calls me "Wildflower."

When I first wrote away for reservations, we were told there were no rooms available at the Sharrow Bay Hotel in Ullswater; but I wrote again to the two gentlemen that owned the estate to please find us a room—pleading that I was a concert pianist and writer and my husband was a poet and educator. Appealing to their romantic spirit did the trick, and we soon found ourselves in the room called "Maria" in the gatehouse, with cows lowing in the meadows underneath our windows, English cabbage-rose chintz draperies and bedspread, potpourri in the drawers, books on the local flora and fauna by the bedside, fresh nosegays on the dresser, and bed linens fit for a royal couple. I remember it all because the exquisite details moved me to paint every last item. Two pages are discreetly clipped together, because when I caught a glimpse of myself reflected in a gilded Edwardian mirror, sitting on the edge of a claw-footed tub, surrounded by rosy wallpaper, as though I were the subject of a Renoir painting, I asked Ernest to hand me my paints and did a little self-portrait. Our idyllic stay at Sharrow Bay was the highlight of our trip, but the journal pages that follow record superlative experiences at Stonehenge, where Ernest's poem was written in a shaky hand, tremulous from his deep emotions, and in the Cotswolds, where we trudged along footpaths, through cow pastures, beside ponds in Upper and Lower Slaughter, and did "B & B" with a couple we remember as "the Blighs."

All around us folks were snapping off photos, and I am sure they were as eager as we to preserve their experiences. But I believe our two little journals are evocative in ways a photo could never be, and it was the beginning of a wonderful ritual that accompanied every trip we ever took. I feel as though we are in the company of such luminaries as Henry James, whose published Italian diaries are illuminated by the watercolors of J. M. W. Turner and John Ruskin; or Lewis and Clarke, who chronicled their travels in nature. A few years ago I discovered the delightful watercolor travel journals of Prince Charles. I was so surprised at the high quality of his work, complete with his remarks about the Scottish highlands and English country estates, that I wrote him a congratulatory note, along with some observations about keeping diaries, and enclosed my little chronicle of my New York debut recital. I received a warm reply, "on behalf of" the Prince of Wales, from the Lord Chancellor of the Exchequer from Buckingham Palace! My favorite example of travel journals are Felix Mendelssohn's letters, which were *like* diaries: punctuated with both his own watercolor sketches of the landscapes he visited and his notations of musical motifs inspired by the scenery.

Twenty years after we were married, Ernest and I went to Oregon, where I was invited to present a lecture-recital at the piano festival at Portland State University and to speak about my new book. I was introduced to Geneva Wright, a pianist, teacher, and watercolorist. Subsequently we found that we were also both rare birds of a vanishing species—we loved to write real letters in longhand. We embarked on a surprisingly frequent and engaging correspondence, sometimes embellishing our missives with watercolor sketches. It is surprising to meet a complete stranger who soon becomes a good friend, but that's exactly what happened. We also found out in the course of our correspondence that each of us had, for years, been keeping travel journals.

A year after our visit to Oregon, Geneva and I decided to meet in Washington, D.C., with our husbands, and she suggested that we each bring along one of our travel journals to share with the other. I leafed through the dozen or so of my journals, packed with some of the most successful paintings I have done, trying to select the very best one to take along to represent my style of journal-keeping.

I picked an especially inspired record of a trip to Wyoming—the Grand Tetons and Yellowstone Park—containing sketches of meadows rampant with wildflowers; mountain peaks in the background; wildlife, including buffalo, foxes, elk, deer, otters, ravens, and songbirds; the Snake River, with its drying bed of colored pebbles; inns; restaurants; and individual specimens of flora and fauna. The rarified mountain air rendered me breathless and I was awestruck by the landscape, but I doggedly kept on painting.

I never get over the manifold pleasures of keeping a journal: there is the peace and delight of sitting on a meadow surrounded by flowers with their heady aromas, laying paint in glistening pools on blinding white paper, while my beloved husband sits nearby reading a book or writing. Then comes the pleasure after I am at home of rereading the diary and reliving the experience. I can conjure up the total environment: the scent of the meadows, the song of the meadowlark, the colors of the sky, the chill in the air, the rate at which the breeze and sun dried the aquarelle, just from beholding the sketch.

I love sharing my journals with certain friends; invariably they languish over each page with the vicarious wonder of how it felt to be there writing and painting, entirely at peace. This particular western journal recorded our drive from Salt Lake City to Jackson Hole, first passing the clay-red mesas and canyons, going through the plains with wild, frolicking pronghorn sheep, and then finally getting that first thrilling glimpse of the snow-capped peaks as they began to appear on the distant horizon. I sketched fast as the car whizzed along, and the journal records the slow metamorphosis of the terrain, until we were bowled over by the majesty of the mountain ranges. My little paintings are annotated by exclamations such as "Wow!" or "Can you believe this?"

I might have selected the journals from two separate trips to Italy, with sketches of Venice, Tuscany, Rome, and Umbria; or the journals from several trips to France, including Paris and its environs, and Monet's gardens at Giverny; or our honeymoon books from England and Scotland. I might have brought along the sketchbooks of the shores, beaches, and gardens around Long Island where we live. But I chose the Wyoming journal because it was infused with an ecstasy that was reflected in an illuminated palette with joyful dancing gestures of the brush. That same journal also contained paintings from a subsequent trip to Seattle, Mt. Rainier, and the Pacific Northwest.

We met our friends at our hotel in D.C., had dinner there, and shared our respective sketchbooks at the table. Geneva's sketchbook was small and refined, with excellent architectural renderings of buildings and monuments and lovely detailed landscapes. My style is looser, quicker, more careless and passionate. We admired and discussed the work we each had done, especially enjoying the shared endeavor and the differences in our styles and approaches.

After dinner we hopped in a cab and went to the theater. Three of us sat in the back of the cab, and my husband sat up front with the driver. After the theater, as we were just about to flag another taxi, my husband suddenly realized that he did not have the tote bag with my journal in it, and we all ran back into the theater to look for it. Soon he became certain that he had left it in the front of the cab that had brought us to the theater, and we all put our heads together to try to remember the name of the cab company, or even the color of the vehicle that had driven us in the dark. We soon found out that there are over two hundred cab companies in Washington, D.C., not to mention independent drivers, and there are no identification cards posted in the cab as there are in New York City taxis. Neither could any of us swear to the exact color of the cab. We could only recall the driver as foreign, possibly from Bangladesh.

The prognosis was bleak, and the enormity of the situation was slowly overtaking me like a lava flow. I exercised extreme self-control to keep from crying, even though I began to tremble at the thought that my precious book might be lost. I was with the three people in the world who probably understood more than anyone else what a loss it would be to me: Geneva, who knew the joys of keeping a journal as well as I, and our two loving husbands, who knew how much our books meant to us.

I did not lose hope. After all, the driver knew where he had picked us up and where he dropped us off, and we had three more days in Washington before we would have to leave. We called the central agency for all cab companies, reporting the missing journal with the director of the lost-and-found; we notified the concierge of the hotel as well as the manager of the theater, in case the book was returned to either of those spots. I realized with horror that I had never written my name and address inside the journal in case it was ever lost. That thought would have been beyond my worst nightmare.

I could not even grieve to the extent that I was suffering, because I knew my poor husband, who had been in charge of the bag, was suffering even more than I, if that were possible. I woke up each morning with a hollow, miserable feeling, before I even remembered why, and as the days went by, I realized I probably would never see my precious little book again: the tote bag was a beautiful item in itself, and there were fine leather gloves inside. Images of the book being tossed into a dumpster by the cabbie as a simple meaningless notebook and the bag and gloves being brought home as trophies to his wife were slowly and insidiously superimposing themselves over any more hopeful outcomes.

We had to leave Washington, and deposited our name and address with several agencies that promised to contact us in the event that my lost treasure turned up. A day after we came home I faxed a flyer with huge letters stating "$500 REWARD for the return of a journal containing original watercolor sketches, great personal value," etc.

I think it was about four months before I was able to acknowledge to myself (after countless calls to the Taxi Commissioner) that the dumpster scenario was probably the exact fate of my journal. (I would gladly have rummaged in the filthiest dumpster, myself, in order to rescue the book.)

The oddest thing was that it felt as though I had lost a dear person. My daughter suggested that perhaps the experience was meant as a lesson "from the universe" in learning how to "let go" and to accept loss, and that perhaps this would serve as preparation for worse losses in life to come. As awful as it may sound to those who may not understand, this irretrievable loss felt as huge as *any* that might befall me. I do not share the view that the universe has its own ways of teaching; I like to believe that we are each very much the captains of our own fates, and in this case, we were simply too careless with something quite precious. All I knew is that I had an enormous hole in my heart, and I had to do mind-over-matter exercises to carry on with daily routines and try to get beyond it. Only my husband sensed when it was overtaking me, and then I tried to shield him from it, as he felt so guilty and responsible. If I didn't love him as much as I do, I might have been relentlessly incriminating.

A year later, my good friend Brent, from Alpine, Wyoming, whose gardens, restaurant, and inn were represented in my journal, and to whom I had sent laser copies of those particular pages, sent me, in turn, copies of his copies, as small recompense for the fifty still-missing pages. They arrived like long-lost ghosts of my work, and I am grateful for his thoughtfulness. It is something retrieved, and better than nothing.

What I learned was to write my name into every journal, to trust no one but myself, and that it is possible to mourn the loss of a material thing as deeply as if it had been alive.

Portrait at the Piano

MY friend Mary and I discovered some years ago that we enjoy engaging in parallel play. She has sometimes come over to my house with her paints and pads and sketched as I practiced. Hours would pass without a word, as we each most happily engaged in our individual pursuits, a magical artistic aura hanging over us. Our friendship is based on a kind of Zen worship of beauty, especially the lovely accidental irregularities borne of humanness. That form of beauty applies itself to the lush postimpressionist canvases she paints, to the music I make, to remnant bolts of fabric that one of us finds and shares with the other or a chunky piece of pottery with an imperfect glaze.

I am most grateful for the capacity to appreciate beautiful things that transcend the material into the spiritual realm. But knowing Mary has extended and sometimes challenged my conceptions of beauty. One day when we were driving somewhere, I chanced to lament the construction of a huge power plant on a meadow that had formerly been a nature conservancy. Mary replied quietly, "Do you know the paintings of Feininger and Burchfield? That's just another form of beauty." Yes, I do know their work; hers was the response of a *provocateuse* and teacher. Indeed, the juxtaposition of industry against nature is a powerful force. I still could not apply the word beauty to those forces, but thenceforth, I saw that power plant in a new way.

For several years Mary has been dealing with an illness that has made it increasingly difficult for her to paint. During one patch of inactivity I was struck with an idea that I hoped might jump-start her work; but I had a selfish motive as well, I must admit. I had an overwhelming desire to have a painting of myself at the piano in my living room, in the manner of my favorite artist, Edouard Vuillard. His subjects always seem to me to be completely and comfortably ensconced in their surroundings, often barely distinguishable against the backdrops of their wall-papers and draperies. It's exactly how harmonious I feel among my own things, and although it might sound vain, I have men-tally superimposed myself upon the images of Misia Nathanson at her piano as painted by Vuillard.

Nobody could have effected this commission better than Mary, whose interior paintings have as much charm and charac-ter as anyone's.

"Mary," I told her, "I have X amount of dollars that I can afford to pay you to paint a picture of me at the piano at home. Mull it over and let me know what you think."

Mary is attached to her paintings like offspring. She prices them high, as though she'd really prefer not to sell them, nor does she need to in order to live well. I never considered her prices outrageous. First, I believe in her great talent, and second, pricing is a very subjective thing: each artist must determine what she thinks her work is worth, independent of others' opin-ions or market trends. Mary's ego is one of the healthiest I know. She is impervious to outer influences and doesn't have to prove anything to herself or to anyone else. That's one of the qualities I admire in her and keep striving for myself.

Mary came back a few days later with her counterproposal: "I'll do the project, but for $XX" (twice the amount), "and if you don't like the results, you don't have to take it."

I had a lot to think about. It was much more money than I had for a project that was arguably a frivolous indulgence. I had become obsessed with the idea, though, and I knew secretly I would find a way to pay for it. But I had concerns about how I would handle it if I did not like the results, without hurting Mary; at the same time I felt certain I *would* like it. I told her I could only do it if I could pay for it in installments from my teaching income. We had a deal.

The nicest thing about this risky business proposition between friends was the work. A cozy atmosphere pervaded the room. I had a concert to prepare for, and she sat near me, with a view of the room, the piano, the windows facing the garden beyond, the oriental carpet with its apple-green field: the makings of a wonderful composition. I was hardly aware of her as I practiced.

She made several sketches, and in the weeks ahead I was increasingly excited and impatient to see the results. When Mary finally called for the unveiling, I became quite nervous. But our history of honesty assuaged any anxieties about handling whatever situation presented itself.

I loved many things about the portrait, primarily the ingratiating and natural posture and gesture of the pianist suggestive of my way at the instrument, the sense of comfort on the bench and at the keyboard, and the pared-down rendering of the essential elements of the room. But the painting was much smaller than I'd anticipated, with a deep pink wall behind the pianist (my walls are white to accommodate the art that hangs on them). When I gently asked Mary about that color, she replied simply that she felt the painting required it. I like deep pink, but not on my walls. My biggest objection, though, was the size of the piano. My piano is just under seven feet long, a beautiful black stodgy thing from the 1920s, big and grand, the most imposing thing in the room. Maybe pianists' egos are somehow involved with the sizes of their pianos; goodness knows that since I got mine, I've always felt it to be an extension of myself. Now I was experiencing a physical repulsion at seeing it foreshortened almost to toy piano proportions. It was that element that prompted me to suggest, again gently, "Mary, the piano is too small. Can you make it larger?"

"No," she answered. "This is the painting. If you don't like it, remember you don't have to take it. I am, by the way, almost finished with a second version from a different sketch, and you might like that one better."

I felt torn between my responses and her feelings. And I felt even more conflicted when she brought me the second painting. This canvas was bigger, the piano was bigger, but the pianist was stiffer, lacking the spontaneity and freedom of the figure in the first sketch. After long deliberation with myself, I chose the second one, with some trepidation and difficulty, because the proportions were truer, even though the pleasure of playing was not as well captured as in the first painting.

The piece hung in various spots on the wall, never seeming completely at home, nor was I with it. I felt less than fulfilled for the money I was spending, and I chalked it up to a bad policy of doing business with friends.

A few months later my husband and I attended a gallery opening in which Mary was showing four works. I was taken aback and chagrined to see the smaller portrait of me at the piano, hanging on the gallery wall, for sale at a pretty price. I felt smitten with a sense of instant recognition: this painting was *me*—the hands, the tilt of the head, the entire attitude, had everything the other painting lacked, and considerations of pink walls and piano size fell to relative unimportance. I remembered what an art teacher once told me: that sometimes when a finished painting does not match preconceived expectations, the best idea is to put the piece away for a while until the original intentions are forgotten. Only then can it be seen objectively at face value. The same rule applies to music. I often wait several weeks before listening to a tape of one of my concerts, because immediately after the event I am only concerned about what might not have matched my original intentions; in fact, the merits of the performance are only clear to me after I have forgotten my plans, and frequently I hear in the tape happy accidents that I had never counted on but that, in fact, had enhanced the performance.

Seeing Mary's painting in the gallery setting, I was overwhelmed by a proprietary feeling and terrified at the thought that the piece might be sold to a stranger. I knew at once that I had chosen the wrong painting, and I felt a desperate urgency to rectify my error before I had lost my chance forever.

I approached Mary and ventured, "Mary, I must talk to you! Now that I see the painting after the several months I've lived with the other, I realize that I chose the wrong one. Would you agree to let me run home, get the one on my wall, and switch it fast before the show gets under way? It will be hardly noticeable to anyone but you and me. The gallery will be glad to have the larger one."

Mary did not return a single word or facial expression. I blathered on. "You *did* give me my choice—you *do* want me to have the one I'm happiest with, don't you?"

Mary and I have shared thirty years of music and art, but we have fundamentally disparate personal styles. Anyone may easily know my feelings as I express them freely; Mary is more taciturn. I don't know what I expected her to say, but I didn't expect "Don't pressure me," uttered with unmistakable finality and coldness. I walked aimlessly around the gallery, stealing intermittent glances at "my" portrait. My husband tried to guide me out of there, but I made another feeble attempt to discuss the painting with her, receiving yet another rebuke.

I left the gallery feeling quite sad and stuck with my own erroneous judgment, secretly wishing that if she was successful in selling her work in the show, that no one buy that particular piece. Ordinarily I'd have hoped for her success in selling every single painting. The situation was hurtful and confusing after so many years of friendship. I tried to explain it to myself in terms of her artistic prerogative to leave the work in the show and not make waves with the gallery owner. I wondered if her firm stand was a sort of redress for my less than ecstatic response to our transaction.

Nothing seemed to justify the lack of communication between us. I realized that my sadness had turned into anger, which kept me from calling Mary during the duration of the exhibit, an unprecedented length of time.

I couldn't deny my curiosity about the fate of the painting, but I refrained from inquiries, trying my best to put the whole episode out of my mind. Eventually I became resigned that the portrait of myself had probably ended up in some stranger's home and I would never see it again.

One day, about a month after the show had closed, my doorbell rang and there was my old friend, Mary, with the painting. We didn't really have to say anything— she simply went over to the wall, took one down, and put the other one up. It's a great little painting; she knew it from the start, and I didn't.

The Green Bowl

I COME home from visiting the Japanese wing of a museum, with its subtle plainness that the Japanese call *shibui,* or the Frank Lloyd Wright room at the Metropolitan Museum of Art, and I want to rid myself of every single extraneous molecule in our home. What follows are heated debates with myself on the subject of collecting: materialism versus spirituality, acquisitiveness versus austerity, cluttered versus pristine, indulgence versus asceticism. I think I have finally resolved a lot of these issues, at least to the extent that I can rationalize not only my love and appreciation for a beautiful ceramic pot, but also the delight of acquiring it.

Addressing the dichotomies in order, I believe that the material thing does not preclude its spiritual values. The properties of humanness as reflected in an imperfect glaze, an irregular shape, a chip, a flaw, are evidence of the uniqueness of us all, a concept I cherish whether it be in music-making, pottery, or all the rest of life. If I can acquire a piece with the beauty of an ancient Korean pot, at a tiny fraction of the price, without taking anything away from anyone, why not? No one will likely love and care for that pot as I would do. So what if I have twenty or thirty pots of similar glaze and character? They speak to each other and to me. Thomas Ladd, a potter in Rhode Island, told me he is attracted

161

to "the intimate human scale of fired clay objects and how they integrate into people's lives." His pitcher, with its jaunty tilt and witty toucan-billed spout, serves us well daily from our counter. A friend of mine called Ladd's chubby little teapot, also in frequent use, "a cunning little pot."

The potter explained, "Weathered rock becomes clay, which can then be hand-formed, then transformed by our kiln, back into rock. Stoneware encapsulates the hand and heart of the potter." When the hands and the heart belong to either of my talented potter-friends, Linda Waits or Lillian Dodson, the pieces takes on even deeper meaning. And it is precisely the hand and heart of the potter that I experience each time I cup my hands around the magnificent Pueblo bowl signed by Ethel Youvella from Tewa village, given to us as a wedding present by dear friends. It was the initiation of our modest collection of Native American pots, which are grouped together in one corner of our dining room. I often feel their vibrations with the power of an entire tribe.

I could never abide clutter, nor would I ever allow the house to feel crowded with objects. I routinely stalk around with a vengeance, organizing, straightening, and removing all nonessential items, including pots. I may subtract something that other folks have generously chosen for us, gifts they thought would fit in but honestly don't. The ones that survive have their own place. They all resonate together, harmonious and organic. The green pottery on our kitchen shelves sends out echoes.

"Uh oh!" my husband usually says whenever I attend a crafts fair or gallery and linger too long. But happily, I have been able to exercise more and more restraint. I have become more discriminating, almost flaunting my self-control when I come home empty-handed. Ascetic I am not, nor ever will be, although (except for the kitchen), I am down to one pot per surface.

When my husband and I left on a trip to Holland, he made his perfunctory pronouncement: "We're not going there to shop." I concurred, but this time he added, "You buy it, you carry it." I fully intended to comply.

One morning in Amsterdam, we found ourselves utterly lost while searching for the Mondrian Museum, so we stopped in to one of the few commercial establishments on that street to ask directions. It was an interior design shop, and while my husband consulted a map with the saleswoman, I browsed around, a dangerous pastime. It was a nice showroom, and I almost got through it unscathed, when something seemed to call to me from a corner of the shop. There on a table was the most wonderful green bowl I had ever seen. It had bountiful proportions, huge in fact, and the glaze had been allowed to drip down along the sides, creating a few happy accidents in its coloration. Here I have to acknowledge that I have plenty of bowls; there seems to be a special emotional component in their attraction for me: possibly something maternal, generous, comforting, copious in the shape.

I told myself that this bowl would undoubtedly be much too costly, which would have cured me on the spot. I never even considered its weight, and I could not walk away from it. It was completely compelling. I sauntered over to the saleswoman, still consulting the map with my husband, and said to her, "You may be about to witness the demise of a beautiful marriage when I ask you this question."

Ernie looked perplexed. He probably never really knows what to expect from me, but this time he may have had an inkling.

I gritted my teeth and asked, "How much is that green bowl over there?" I expected to hear a very high price, and was halfway between hoping for and against it.

The price she quoted in guilders came to an amazingly low forty dollars. I was divested of my last defense against buying it.

"Carol . . . no," Ernie ventured. "Remember, you carry it." I hadn't even lifted it. Weight had not been a factor. Aesthetics ruled. They always do.

"Will you take an American Express check?"

"No, I am sorry. Only Dutch currency," she apologized. "But there is a bank a few blocks from here, and I can wrap it up for you while you get the money."

"Fine. Ernie, will you at least walk with me to the bank?"

"What ever happened to our trip to the Mondrian Museum? And what will you do with another green bowl? And are you prepared to carry it around all day? Because I am not touching it."

"Yes, Ernie, I am prepared to carry it around." (I cast a surreptitious glance at the enormous object.) "It is not just another green bowl. It is a remarkably beautiful bowl, and I cannot walk away from it."

When we returned from the bank, the woman had surrounded it with bubble wrap, brown paper, and rope, and she even had attached a handle. I lifted it. It was positively leaden, but I made not a grimace, nor let a complaint nor whine nor whimper pass my lips. I accepted my penance.

I walked around Amsterdam from the museum to a restaurant and finally back to our hotel near the Concertgebuow. I had carried it with my right arm, with my left arm, with both arms across my chest as if it were a baby. I would have borne it on my back or worn it on my head, and I think I may have done permanent damage to my tendons and muscles; it might even be the source of the chronic muscle spasm in my trapezius I get to this day. I still had to climb the four flights up the narrow staircase to our garret apartment, which I did, stoically, under my husband's scolding, unsympathetic eye.

A couple of days later when we were packing to leave for home, my husband quietly asked me how I was planning to manage my two carryons plus the bowl.

For reply, I laid open my suitcase, dumped out all the contents on the bed, and lined the bag with my thickest articles of clothing. I took the bowl out of its wrapping and set it on top, filling it with nightgowns, underwear, blouses; and lo! the suitcase zipped up around it all. The bag was barely budgeable, but it had wheels, and somehow, step by step, I was able to descend the four flights, gingerly, to the curb where the cab awaited. The driver lifted the valise into the trunk with a scathing glance at me, as though to ask, *Is it filled with rocks?* I affected an innocent, vacant countenance in response.

By some miracle, both the bowl and I made it home unscathed. As tired as I was, I quickly unpacked, removed the prized bowl, and set it ceremoniously upon our antique pine kitchen table. My husband regarded me with a look I could not fathom.

I mumbled, "For fruit, or mail—anything we want to put in it."

Still he kept staring at me without a response.

"You are thinking," I continued, "that I am an incorrigible, acquisitive, spoiled woman, and you don't understand what I saw in this bowl."

"I am thinking," my husband replied, "that you are the most stubborn, determined, astonishing, and beautiful woman I have ever known, and that you were right. It *is* a wonderful bowl."

The Lost Concert

IN Room 563 I am trying desperately to concentrate on the Sinfonia to the Bach C Minor Partita that is going round and round in my head above the din of the corridor: a morbid, high-speed cortège of nurses, aides, orderlies pushing gurneys, doctors, and visitors all rushing past my open door. On the other side of the curtain, a sick old woman whines pitifully in her bed, and I try to comfort her with words that seem to have no meaning, especially in concert with her groans and the occasional shrieks of pain from across the hall.

My left wrist, shunted with an IV needle taped into my vein, is faintly flexing with the *portato* bass line of the Andante. Both inner elbows are bruised and bandaged from the countless vials of blood that have been drawn every few hours. My fingers are sore from frequent stabbings to test blood-sugar levels. I am being "observed" after a one-in-a-thousand complication from what should have been a routine procedure. I have lost a great deal of blood, and instead of being glad I am alive, all I can think about are my poor fingers, hands, and arms and the lecture-recital I am scheduled, publicized, and committed to give in six days. Even if they ever check me out of this hospital, will I ever regain enough stamina to perform?

I have suffered occasional cancellations due to snow emergencies, but never, in over fifty years of playing publicly, have I had to cancel for reasons of health. *Pianists are humans too* is one refrain ringing through my ears. The other is, *I can do this thing—the show must go on.* Then I remember a train ride into New York City, followed by a taxi to Carnegie, filled with anticipation at hearing the great pianist Radu Lupu. Plastered diagonally across the huge photo of his bearded image was the shocking word CANCELED. Aside from the great disappointment that I along with 2700 others felt, I was greatly concerned because I knew that he had rehearsed in the hall earlier that day. When I spoke to him the next day, he was still quite sick with a stomach flu, lamenting his decision to cancel his only New York recital that season. Even a globetrotting pianist like Radu, who is inured to the reality that travel and the incredibly hard work of touring will take their toll, feels the weight of that responsibility. Of course, he has the opportunity to do the program a few days later for another and yet another audience.

For a pianist like me with a scaled-down career, the thought of a cancellation takes on particularly devastating proportions. Questions that border on being silly flood in: for example, *How can I contact everyone with a ticket?* My tendency would be to put everyone else's convenience before my own health. That kind of thinking is probably symptomatic of a more serious syndrome than my physical illness. My friend Lillie, a nurse who has offered unstinting support and succor, reminds me that we are all products of a generation brought up with a modicum of guilt and the dictum that we must never put ourselves first. Indeed, I am more likely to identify with an artist like André Watts, who went onstage in New York the day after he told me on the phone that he had pneumonia; he is also known to have resumed a concert tour only three months after suffering a brain hemorrhage.

Rationally, I am fully aware how easily the world could get along without this concert of mine, and that knowledge alone assuages my agitation and gives me momentary peace. I know that if need be, I will have the courage to cancel. Meanwhile, with two entirely separate programs to give within a month, I close my eyes and run through the music in my head to assure myself that it is all still there, intellectually, even if my physical stamina is diminishing rapidly. The second day, when things get worse, I tearfully call my colleagues Jean and Lucille, who have a four-hand piano program under their twenty fingers. I ask them whether they can stand by and step in for me if need be, and they readily agree. My mind is spinning with options: I am certain that even if I could, conceivably, be out of the hospital in time to give the concert myself, I probably should not push myself; I should call the hall and offer them the choice of postponing the event or accepting the alternative concert. Most enigmatically, the thought of handing over this plum grieves me, but in my weakened state, it also offers great relief.

After a considerable loss of blood and three days of nothing to eat or drink, I am released from the hospital. The joy of being at home with Ernie buoys my spirits almost to manic proportions, and I begin to think that even though I am beyond fatigued, I probably have enough principal in the bank, technically, to do the concert without too much practicing. The moment I express these thoughts, I am bombarded with warnings and admonitions from everyone from my mother (*You're not thinking of going through with your concert, are you?* uttered in a tone implying that only a crazy woman would) to well-meaning nonmusician friends who have no clue as to what canceling would feel like. Even pianist-friends, who understand the concern that we not be thought "capricious or unreliable" (as Geneva Wright put it), try to remind me that canceling would not be the end of the world, and that heroism is never fully appreciated anyway.

In the past, I have returned to teaching only days after major surgery, a broken leg, and all manner of tragic loss. Teaching is theraupeutic, and my students have proven, again and again, how caring they are. In that case, it is not a question of heroics but, rather, some kind of ethic of productivity that makes me detest giving in to something, anything, rather than pulling myself together as soon as possible.

A concert is another story: playing the piano is much more physical than anyone who doesn't do it imagines. You don't just sit there and "tickle the ivories," to quote the world's most idiotic description of what we pianists do. Arthur Rubinstein once suggested that if we "expressed" on an inanimate, unyielding table what we "do" on a live piano, the amount of visceral energy consumed in the process would be readily apparent to the stunned observer. Someone even once calculated the impressive number of calories consumed in an hour of work at the piano.

Three days before the concert, still in a state of denial, I am thinking I might be able to pull it off and am on the verge of letting my "subs" know I would do the gig myself. Two days before the concert, my body goes into a shocklike state, weakened and traumatized, leaving no doubt even in my own denying-idiot's mind that I simply *cannot* do it. At this point, too weak even to fully experience the disappointment I know I must be feeling, I call my patient pianist-friends for the last time with my final dreaded decision.

This is a complex moment: undeniable feelings of failure and defeat are accompanied by a curious sense of weightlessness. I feel I have grown up in some strange way. I have been reminded that I am not indispensable, that the world will not cave in around me, and that there was no need to prove my invincibility and jeopardize my life. My friend Judy gently reminds me, "Anyone who knows you, knows you would have dragged yourself onstage half-dead, if you could have." Most important, I have learned that I care about myself.

From the Porch

WHEN I was a young girl, my parents bought a little cottage in a lakeside community upstate. There was nothing luxurious about the village or the bungalow, but I have some very fond memories of the place, mostly associated with my sense of smell and the song of the birds.

The air was imbued with the smell of the earth, especially when it rained. From the tiny screened porch, I could smell the damp soil coming up through the floor and the chlorophyll from the woods around the house. There was room for only the daybed and a little table, but with its potpourri of faint mustiness, a woody essence tinged with wafts of freshly mown meadow grasses blowing in from the farm down the road, that mini-porch sometimes seemed like the coziest spot on earth. I dreamed many dreams there and read many books by the wobbly little wall lamp overhead. Chilled by the evening air, I would wait until the last moment to curl up under one of my mother's hand-crocheted afghans. Occasionally the late afternoon song of a white-throated or song sparrow or the night call of a screech owl made it even more perfect.

It took over forty years to reproduce the pleasures of that heavenly milieu for my adult self to enjoy.

One summer, instead of going away, Ernest and I spent the

money to add a screened porch onto the back of our house. Although it is at least five times bigger than the one of my youth, it has the same rustic qualities and brings me in touch with my greatest pleasures, including all those scents from nature that no *parfumier* has ever managed to quite capture in a bottle.

For three-quarters of the year we live out there on the porch, eat our meals, read the paper, meditate, and watch birds and whatever other creatures scamper onto the property. But one day I realized that our porch had a tragic flaw: no place to nap. We had a great-looking antique wicker chaise left to me by our dear old friend, Nelly, the fairy godmother who brought the two of us together, but it was a singularly uncomfortable thing to recline on. We also had a glider with cedar slats, and any sad sack who might be tempted to lie down on it would be crippled and scarred with deeply barred striations on his back forevermore.

The day I realized that my life's ambition was to take a nap on our porch, between piano lessons, after practicing hard or gardening, and perhaps even over an entire mellow night, I went out on a safari to find a nice second-hand daybed that would weather well outside. After a fruitless search I commissioned our good friend Alan, master woodcraftsman, to build one that I designed. Now we have a nicer one than we ever thought possible, beautifully constructed in an Arts and Crafts style, painted apple green, and I have fulfilled my dream many times over. But the same summer that my dream came true, it was shattered by bad news.

For all the years that I have lived in this house, a certain exquisite tract of woods that links our property to the next has been my focus for meditation and a great source of inspiration. I have always shared the Native American view that we do not own the trees—that they are leased to our loving care for as long as we live with them. I could also call myself a pantheist, if that means worshipping the presence of God in every living plant and animal.

If I were asked to impose the image of the most beautiful place in the world in my mind, I would choose to picture these woods in any season. If I were asked to name the most beautiful music, I would say "the song of the thrush," who must have the protection of deep, old forestation to nest. When my daughter was growing up in our wonderful house, our favorite wake-up alarm was the voice of the thrush. That song was her inspiration for the flute music she was so gifted at producing, as much as it was mine.

I have actually felt the transformation of energy, the synthesizing of the beauty of the woods and of its birdsongs as they metamorphose into music. In reality, those woods were only partially ours; but this has been a neighborhood in which folks have treasured their tranquility, privacy, and life in close proximity to nature. It is precisely because of these undeveloped wooded areas between our homes that we have enjoyed wildlife including pheasants, owls, thrushes, foxes, raccoons, rabbits, wild turkeys, and hawks.

The question is whether anyone has the right to come in and take all that away from anyone else. The people next door (I no longer call them neighbors) sold their house and land to someone who bought it not for the natural beauty, but to subdivide it for a profit. I quickly typed up a petition and walked around the whole area, enlisting names of neighbors who, like us, were horrified at the apparent plans. The subsequent hearings in the town hall yielded limits on just how much of the old forestation the new occupants would be allowed to log, how much of a thicket we could insist upon their leaving between any new building and ours, and how close the new driveway could come to our property line.

However, no matter how we might protest, in the end, people do have the right to do what they would like with a piece of property they have purchased, so long as they stay within the zoning laws. In this case, they were denied the right to build a house on their front lawn, but they could build a house in the back, right in the middle of my favorite wooded tract, and they sold that acre to a builder for an astonishing sum.

We have since realized that many builders belong to a breed born with greed where conscience ought to be. How much house can one builder stuff into one acre? As we watched and listened, one tree after the next screamed its pain and shook the earth as it fell. The builders poured the cement foundation, then they framed it, and every time we thought that was *it,* another higher eave or roof line would be added, until what stands where there used to be woods is a structure we nicknamed "Howard Johnson's." Two years ago we had put in a new window so that we could see more of the woods from our dining room. Now we have the great pleasure of eating and getting an ulcer at the same time.

But I cannot expect sympathy from anyone. Some people remind me of all the years of peace I was so lucky to live with; others caution, "Don't sweat the small stuff"; my husband tells me "not to look over there" and that "if there is nothing we can do, then we have to accept it"; still others remind me of how most of the world lives. I have been trying to stifle my feelings; I almost feel ashamed of my sadness, after being preached to so righteously.

Recent reports that noise pollution has contributed to the decline of the environment have me worried for all forms of wildlife, including myself. I watched a film of various creatures of nature acting in bizarre ways in response to loud noises; a naturalist who records birdsongs in the wild reported that for every unpolluted recorded hour of pure natural "music," he has to waste hundreds of hours waiting for trucks, planes, and other man-made disturbances to subside. He described the increase in predation caused by the fact that noise pollution prevents animals from detecting warning signals. And of course, studies have also picked up evidence of real stress caused to man, by man, in large, noisy cities where folks constantly have their sleep disturbed by sirens, motorcycles, car alarms, garbage trucks, screeching brakes, boom boxes, and so on.

For those reasons we have chosen to live in the country, where nuisance noises come in the form of a bunch of crows (I call them gangsters) chasing a red-tailed hawk, or a screech owl's mournful cry piercing the quiet of the night, or a pair of raccoons making whoopie in the woods. For the last few months, for every hour of pure "natural" music, not to mention my own man-made music, we have suffered hours of bulldozers, carpenters' saws, delivery trucks, cement mixers, and so on. Whoever buys that huge house next door will undoubtedly have three large SUVs and a family of screaming children. Goodbye peace, goodbye privacy on our porch, and goodbye thrush songs, since the thrush requires deeper thickets than the developers left.

But I do have a few friends who understand. I phoned my friend Fiona in Siena, Italy, who, with her husband, fashioned their stone country house from the shell and rubble of an old Tuscan farmhouse, using the original materials. They share our aesthetic and style of living and treasure their privacy and ability to garden in peace, and she told me that it is happening everywhere: the little farm belonging to their late neighbor, Ottorino, who drowned in his own well, had been sold and divided. "You will just have to plant lots of trees," she instructed.

So I appealed to my friend Joan McGillicuddy, a landscape designer and a treasure, who came over, took some photos, and reassured me, "This is the winter, Carol. You will be surprised how the spring foliage will change things, and I will find trees and shrubs that will fare well in the shade, that will grow fast, and bring you back the pleasure of your garden."

I bless her for her optimism and the hope she has given me. Indeed, this past spring, as the leaves in the thicket unfurled and the few new Leyland cypresses, viburnum, and rhododendrons were planted, the blow was softened and my ire has been quelled. Joan's newly designed grove of shrubs almost obliterates the house for three seasons out of the year, and I have hopes that over time the evergreens' growth will further improve the situation.

The other day I came across a piece of stone garden statuary that was not only beautiful, but a symbolic icon. The sculpture represents Pan, the engaging mythological faun. He is playing his syrinx, the multitubed reed flute of various pitches, named after the larynx of birds. The blithe-spirited little sprite has one cloven hoof lifted as in a dance step to his own piping. This wonderful statue depicts in stone the exact atmosphere described musically by Claude Debussy in his evocative flute soliloquy *Syrinx*, my daughter's favorite flute piece as she was growing up.

I have placed Pan in the middle of my perennial garden, which is on the same trajectory as the intrusive house if I look over from my porch, or from my windows. The statue and the surrounding flowers draw my eye, make me smile, and evoke the spirit of the thrush's song mixed with Kim's flutings, and together with the breezes, that's a perfect lullaby for me.

The Diverse and Controversial Uses of the Indispensable Black Marker

I AM the champion wielder of markers, and I have several from fine to broad for any conceivable use, from frivolous to serious. Maybe I inherited that talent from my father, who related how, as an underprivileged child, he would color in his legs and feet wherever they showed through the holes in his socks. I have used hundreds of black markers over the years for concert flyers for myself and other musicians, when the alternative would have been no publicity at all. I have used my black markers to fill in the gougings on the fallboards of my black pianos from my fingernails or those of my students, or where I have tapped a pencil to keep them in strict tempo, causing the ebonized veneer to chip off and expose the bare wood.

Tacked onto my bulletin board is a faded photo of a class of about fifteen piano students posed around a Steinway grand, with my first teacher, Esther Bernstein, smiling proudly in their midst on the stage. Sitting on the floor in front of the older students are a few younger ones, and there's the smallest of them all: myself at six, sprawling casually, all limbs, elbow on knee, chin cupped in palm, in an exceedingly unladylike posture.

My mother would blush if she saw this old photo—the dress hiked high, exposing my skinny bare legs right on the stage in front of the whole audience! I open my desk drawer to get a permanent black magic marker and carefully and deliberately draw a new, more modest hemline, covering the bareness, as though I could ever undo an indiscretion perpetrated so many years ago. As though a six-year-old could be capable of an indiscretion.

Somewhere in the sloppy archival realms of my basement and attic there are recordings too from those early days that my father made on an early wire disc recorder. He took the performances off of the radio or television or backstage in the small halls—wherever it was arranged that I had a little recital. The photo conjures up a faint, indescribable melancholy, the sweet strains of remembrance of my first public appearances in those inno-cent, stress-free early forays before the public: Chopin's "Minute" Waltz, C. P. E. Bach's *Solfeggietto,* little Grieg pieces, a Haydn concerto. I can recall peering through the curtains from the wings, wearing a little dotted Swiss dress with smocking, bought for me by my doting teacher, partly out of love, partly because she thought my parents might not have been able to buy me a fancy new recital dress; but somehow they got me a baby grand piano because they recognized my needs at an early age, after I had begun picking out tunes on my grandfather's upright.

In those days I was so anxious for my turn to go out onto the stage, play my pieces, then be turned with my back to the key-board, as my teacher demonstrated my perfect pitch, bidding me identify the tones and chords as they were struck. The bliss of in-nocence. Now, as much as I love and need to perform, that walk from the green room to the piano always seems like the last mile.

Fifty years after that early photo was taken, the father of one of my students took a similar photo of my own piano class gathered around me after their recital. They range in age from twelve to sixty, and the photo reflects the elation and relief after their perform-ances; but the first thing that caught my eye was a slight, unwelcome little jowl on my face that most assuredly had to go. I opened my desk drawer for my trusty marker and drew in my idea of an ideal taut jawline, filling in the new silhouette with black, chuckling at the improvement in my image.

"Why do you do that, Mom?" my son, Dennis, once asked with the unmistakable tone of consternation. "So many of your photos have a strange black touch-up marks."

"It's cheaper than plastic surgery, and it makes me happier, honey. Just chalk it up to your mother's eccentricity or vanity."

One time, at the last minute before leaving the house to give a concert, I glanced in the mirror and noticed for the first time that within the print of my long floral dress with its black background was a particularly gaudy-colored flower placed squarely over one breast, calling undue attention, I thought, to that part of my anatomy. Very quickly I opened my desk drawer, got out one of my reliable markers, unzipped the dress enough to lay the top part on the table, colored over the bright offending bloom, got back into the dress, and left for the hall, happier. I felt so happy and relieved, in fact, that it was one of my rare concerts without nerves. (Later that evening, however, I was startled to discover a black "blemish" on my breast that I feared was a rare instant form of cancer, until I remembered having donned the altered concert attire while the black ink was still wet.)

It seems that my son, as a direct descendant of my father and me, inherited the talent for marking. When he was a teenager, he had to produce a concert photo for a newspaper article with no time to take new ones. He rummaged through boxes of photos and came up with a fine one of himself playing his cello. The one small problem was that he was stripped from the waist up. Undaunted, he took typewriter correcting fluid and painted a deep white V to represent the shirt. Then with bold strokes, using a permanent black marker, he painted in the bow tie and jacket, and voila! instant tux. We could defy anyone to guess the tailor of his custom-made concert "attire."

I have described some of the odd and sundry ways a musician with a whole set of black markers can apply them; but the day I was invited to perform a Mozart concerto of my own choice with a chamber orchestra, my marker met its finest hour, accomplishing its most serious task: I decided to write my own cadenza (using a fine-tipped marker), and as satisfying and challenging a project as that was, it was not without controversy.

I felt like a child in a gumdrop shop considering all my wonderful possibilities. At last I selected K. 488, rolled up my sleeves, and set to the task of making the concerto my own.

I have taught this piece at least a dozen times and demonstrated it well, I think, for my students; but there is an elevated state that transcends mere excellence of execution—a state that evolves from one's own life experience, humility, wonder, and astonishment that any mortal should have left us such a legacy. The longer I spent with this masterpiece and the deeper I probed, the closer I felt I was coming to its core.

Despite the strictures and conventions associated with Mozart performance, from the moment of the piano's first entrance, the pianist can personalize the performance in many ways. Mozart was somewhat lax about notating details, and so through phrasing, nuances of articulation and touch, gradations of dynamics, even a few added embellishments, the pianist enters the realm of creativity. Of utmost importance is the heartbeat—the energy and living spirit of the music that conveys the basic message, which, in the case of K. 488, seems to be joy's triumph over sorrow.

Yet it is in the cadenza that the soloist may take the reigns and make a free flight into fancy, alighting into a realm of unabashed and full-hearted self-expression. Cadenzas are made of "flourishes, inventions, and the execution of spontaneous and elaborately decorative passages," according to *The Oxford Companion to Music*.

Mozart wrote a perfectly fine cadenza for this work. Mozart and Beethoven, who were two of the greatest improvisers of all time, did their best to quell others' attempts to improvise cadenzas to their concertos because they didn't trust anyone else with their own music; hence, they wrote their own cadenzas, often offering several choices to the pianist, to ensure their high quality.

One day, while working on the cadenza that Mozart wrote into the score, I came to the trill in bar 25, and thoroughly infected by the high spirits of the work, I proceeded to improvise an extension to the cadenza, wanting to prolong the unleashed joy of it all, which is so short-lived and then gone forever. It was at that moment that I grabbed a black marker and started jotting down some of my ideas on paper. Composing has never been one of my primal urges; in fact the only writing I ever did was for composition courses as a music major in college. Now so many ideas, in the form of hundreds of black dots, were fairly flying off the end of my marker, and in the end I had a page of writing that seemed to jell. I thought I would like to append it to the Mozart cadenza at the right-hand trill in bar 25.

So I began to practice the composite cadenza, and although it pleased me, I was plagued with my historic self-doubts. God forbid that it be interpreted as an arrogant implication that my own humble efforts deserved to be hyphenated to the master's own. Does the fact that Mozart wrote out the entire cadenza within the movement itself suggest his intention that it remain inviolable? Are we duty-bound to play Mozart's own cadenza centuries later simply because he wrote one? I do not think so. Improvisation is a corollary of imagination, and after abiding by the conventions and strictures to which we reverentially adhere during the work itself, I felt a strong urge to allow my imagination to "fly the coop."

These were my spontaneous responses, and so I took one step closer to a decision and taped my page of black-marker dots into the music.

Several weeks before the concert, I decided to play the cadenza for musicians I respect, and their overwhelming consensus was *Do it!* Then I presumed upon my friendship with André Watts and Radu Lupu, sending them each copies of the page I was adding on. André encouraged me to do my own thing, and when Radu called from Switzerland, we had a protracted discussion on details of phrasing and dynamics. Finally we got to the cadenza. His take was that I either play the Mozart cadenza as is or entirely write my own, instead of appending my piece of writing to Mozart's. I continued to consider the matter, grateful for the rare and wonderful coaching and advice.

The issue of which cadenza to play continued to confound me. I found the original Mozart cadenza to be too short, but I was deeply affected by Radu Lupu's advice and ruled out adding my page onto the Mozart. Another choice might have been to play the Ferruccio Busoni cadenza, which was sent to me by a friend, but I found it to be too florid and out of character. Someone else suggested an Artur Schnabel cadenza. In the end, I ruled out playing *anyone* else's cadenza: once I decided that it would be permissible to substitute some other cadenza for Mozart's, I decided to expand on my own ideas. The moment that decision was made, out came the marker, and after some hard work I came up with two good pages that were not only a little longer than Mozart's one-and-a-half-page cadenza but more fun to play. I had the overwhelming sense that I was paying my own homage to the score all the time I was working on it.

No sooner had I written my cadenza and begun to feel comfortable about using it than I bumped into a friend who is quite a famous pianist backstage at Carnegie Hall. He chanced to ask me whether I had any concerts coming up, and I mentioned the Mozart concerto engagement, which was by then a couple of weeks away. Then I chanced to ask him what he thought of my decision to substitute my own cadenza for the Mozart.

He stepped away from me in horror, as though I had suddenly contracted the plague, exclaiming, "You can't do that! It is written right into the score! I'm sorry you told me you were going to do that!"

I had recurring visions of my laborious musical notations being sucked back into my pen. A few more days filled with self-questioning followed, until I finally related the incident to my friend Jerry Lowenthal.

"Nonsense!" he assured me. "That was the voice of musical fundamentalism, a purist faction that adheres strictly to the rules." Jerry went on to inform me that the pianist Robert Levin believed that Mozart had, in fact, written that cadenza for a poor student, and that one should NOT play it at all. "In other words, you can play any cadenza you want," he urged. (I love Jerry.) "Play your own!"

And so I played my own cadenza, happily, but with a twinge of regret and guilt for the lost Mozart bars. Several weeks after the concert, I was speaking to yet another friend, Paul Schenly, the director of the Cleveland Institute of Music's Piano Department. I thought he would get a kick out of the discussions about the Mozart cadenza, and just out of curiosity, I asked him his opinion.

"Since you are asking me my opinion on a subject where my good friends and colleagues have differing opinions, let me say with an ear for politics, that of course you are ALL correct. Seriously, let me say that I think I could imagine Mozart viewing the situation in the following way: he would have wanted a cadenza to reflect the context of a performance (technical resources, number of players, and so on), and I am sure those considerations still hold true two hundred years later."

Then he added, "Coincidentally, earlier this year I met Charles Rosen at a flea market, and we went over to a piano and spent the morning together talking about Mozart and Beethoven. He mentioned that he was performing the A Major Concerto, K. 488, himself and asked me if I didn't think the cadenza was too short—that he was thinking of adding some measures of his own! So there is yet another vote for your point of view."

Rosen was adding his own bars to Mozart's cadenza! How I wished that I had had that conversation with Paul before my concert. Charles Rosen, the distinguished pianist and scholar, corroborating my own idea, would have given me just the fodder and courage I needed to do what I had truly wanted to do: append some of my own black dots to Mozart's cadenza. Of course, Rosen's pen is less likely to be challenged than Montparker's, and that is one major advantage of a career with a capital C!

An Evening with Beethoven

I REALLY wanted to practice, but Ernie kept calling me to watch a video of *The Sopranos* with him. Nearly everyone we know watches it, and we were curious, so he took it out of the library. I got sucked into the inappropriately affectionate depiction of an Italian mafia family; as it slowly took on its insidiously sinister shade, with rampant killing, I became increasingly tense until I guess I started sighing audibly. Ernie kept looking over at me with concern and suddenly changed the channel, coming upon an orchestra being conducted in a church somewhere. Two bars of music revealed that it was Beethoven's Ninth, first movement, and neither one of us could turn it off. My overwhelming thought was that the two programs represented both extremes of human possibility: *The Sopranos* portrayed the lowest level to which man could sink, and the Beethoven was humanity to the highest.

I couldn't have shared the music with a better person than Ernie. Seeing his sweet gray head nodding and swaying reconfirmed the profound universality of the music: the struggle of the first movement giving way to the humor of the Scherzo; the questions posed in the third movement; and finally, the jubilant triumph of the final movement with chorus. Even a nonmusician must respond.

"I sang in the soprano section of the chorus in college in this symphony," I mumbled. "I accompanied the chorus in rehearsals, and then the orchestra replaced me and I sat in at the concert. We were all hoarse from singing our brains out when it was over."

"I had my whole camp dancing to this music on rainy days," Ernie confessed.

"That's understandable. It makes you want to leap around with joy." I almost got up from the couch to prove my point, but sitting next to my love and listening was too perfect. Our short exchanges were relieved by long periods of rapt attention to the performance.

"Can you tell which church that is by the architecture or the paintings and icons?"

"It looks as though it must be Eastern European. It's almost Byzantine, though."

"Maybe Poland."

I thought to myself, *Ernie is remembering his family members who were killed in Poland by the Nazis.* I looked at his fine profile, his sharply Polish nose, the intelligent high brow with its expressive wrinkles, the crinkles about his eyes, the beautiful head.

"I think the conductor's name is Gilbert something. I've seen him before. He's obviously full of joy, but much too plugged into the score."

"The orchestra looks as though they must have played this work a hundred times. They seem mighty jaded. But you can't spoil this music."

I thought about how much I would have loved to sit and play amidst an orchestra in a masterwork like the Ninth, a joy a pianist never gets. I think I would love to have played the bassoon—especially in this work.

"If you could choose one instrument of the orchestra, Ernie, that you would want to play, which would it be?"

"I don't know. Never thought about it." A long thoughtful silence, and then, "The trumpet."

"That would be my *last* choice. Why the trumpet?"

"Oh, I don't know, Miles or Louis, I guess."

That's what I love about us. We're coming from such different places, but we always meet. Whatever did Miles Davis and Louis Armstrong have to do with Beethoven? But there we were, my feet up on his lap, his hands giving me a great foot massage to Beethoven's Ninth, and each of us enjoying the music with equal fervor.

We both love choral music, especially after chaperoning the prizewinning choir from Ern's high school to Italy and following them around from piazza to piazza, church to church, as their voices echoed through the hallowed vaulted chambers: St. Peter's in Rome, St. Francis of Assisi, and churches in Venice, Spoleto, Ferrara, and Perugia. We swore we would never travel with a hundred teenagers again, nor in *any* group, but it was an unusual perspective of Italy.

The Adagio movement of the Ninth has one of Beethoven's most deeply moving themes, one appropriated by Schumann (in the *Aufschwung,* among other works). Sometimes my feeling of debt to Beethoven for his immeasurable gifts to the world seems more than I can bear without overflowing in tearful frustration that I never can repay it. I think of Schumann's tribute: "Beethoven, into whom God poured enough gifts for a thousand vessels." And yet Beethoven expressed self-doubts about his ability to elevate Schiller's "Ode to Joy" to its deserved heights. He revered the poets Homer and Shakespeare, but Goethe and Schiller were his favorites. Beethoven leapt for joy, himself, when he decided to use the ode to express his own moral conviction that only joy has the power to bond mankind.

Schiller's joyous lines of poetry, first from the bass-baritone, reiterated by the quartet of soloists, then by the choir, would even be more uplifting and convincing if the peoples of the world were not exhibiting such abject hatred.

"It will never happen," murmurs my generally optimistic husband.

"It all seems so hopeless," I echo.

We listen, and sing, and inhale the great music, and I think that if I can manage to shut out the cruel world for these moments, I can indulge my gratitude for how lucky I am to be able to play Beethoven, to teach Beethoven, to share him; then I begin to think how lucky I am to be alive, to live with the person I love, who also loves Beethoven.

Rondo in the Rubble

ICOULD hardly go to the piano to practice, even with a few concerts coming up, much less convince myself that making music was anything more than a trivial pursuit. Indeed, everything that had been rosy and golden before September 11 now felt as though it were covered with soot, including my piano. It was difficult to think about music with the toxic air blowing due northeast from Manhattan, thirty-five miles out to Huntington.

I was teaching when someone called to tell me the awful news, and my student and I stood transfixed with the rest of the world. That day, and in the days that followed, although I made the decision to leave the judgments about lessons to each family, incredibly, not a single student canceled a lesson. They greeted me with warmer-than-ever, almost desperate hugs, and I quickly resolved that at least for the period of each lesson, I would put aside my own feelings (easier said than done) and prove to them that certain events in our lives would not change.

I recounted to my students an interview I had watched of the Dalai Lama in which he was asked how he could still seem so happy, when China had taken over his land, his people, and his resources. His unforgettable answer was, "Yes, they have taken my country, my people, my resources, but they cannot take my happiness." I sat at the piano trying to force out the grim images from my mind, and trying to desist from asking myself who really needs to hear another Mendelssohn *Variations sérieuses* at my next concert. But wasn't it Mendelssohn himself who lamented the inadequacy of words to describe certain emotions, insisting that music was a much more explicit expresser of feelings? Indeed, I find that my available vocabulary is deficient in times like these: the words *awful, horrible, heartsick* don't come near the depths we need. Those feelings for which we cannot find words may find expression only in music. The piano lessons are supreme challenges in the powers of concentration and justification. I have at least been successful in keeping my students focused.

I tried to find insights from other musicians to help myself. The composer Steve Reich, who lives six blocks away from the site of the World Trade Center, stated, "A lot of musicians are asking 'How can I do music now?' I think if that's the way you feel now, there was something wrong with your purpose before. If the seriousness of purpose was there before, it will get you through an emergency now."

I read somewhere that the conductor Edward Polochik had to take a thirty-five-hour bus ride for a performance when his flight out of Baltimore was canceled. "I would have crawled on my hands and knees across broken glass to get here," he told the Associated Press. "As musicians we have a very important tool to help the country move forward. That tool is music. It can help greatly in the healing process."

When John F. Kennedy was gunned down in 1963, Leonard Bernstein conducted not a requiem nor a funeral march, but Mahler's "Resurrection" Symphony. It signaled a resurgence of hope. "Our sorrow and rage will not inflame us to seek retribution; rather they will inflame our art. . . . This will be our reply to violence: to make music more intensely, more beautifully, more devotedly than before."

So what was my problem? About three weeks into the aftermath, perhaps because I needed a lot of support myself, I decided to question some of my students about how or whether their relationships with the piano had changed as a result of the tragedy. I learn so much from my students. Here are some of their comments:

Greta told me, "My Haydn sonata is such a jolly piece. At first I thought, 'This is too happy. How can I play this?' Then I felt, I won't let them intimidate me, nor take this jolly feeling away from me. Besides, I have a teacher who gives me heavy assignments, and I have to do them!"

"In the long run," Paula said, "it has not affected my work at the piano, but I could not play for two weeks. I felt that because for me the piano is such a joyous thing, that it was inappropriate."

Yoshiko told me she could not play for two weeks. "I was too unhappy, and glued to the TV."

Charlotte said she didn't think that the tragedy had changed her relationship with the piano. "My goals are still the same—to accomplish as much as I can. Perhaps if I knew someone personally, I'd be grieving in a different way. This catastrophe is too large for it to sink in."

Ryan, who was only thirteen, claimed, "The piano teaches me concentration and cleans my mind of other things. I guess it depends on what piece I am playing, and what kind of expression it requires."

For Andrea, "The piano is more of a release than ever before. I always went to the piano whenever I was sad or worried; it's helpful to me. It's my fantasy world where I can escape. Chopin or Schubert will be here even if buildings aren't."

"The piano is an oasis for me," Gary told me. "More of a sanctuary than ever before."

Alfie told me he tries "not to think about anything else" when he is at the piano, and he added, "Most of the time I can succeed."

I was afraid to call one of my students, Yuka, who works in the complex of buildings downtown at the Trade Center, but after getting up my courage, I dialed her number on the afternoon of September 11. To my amazement, she answered the phone, quite audibly shaken. "Ms. Montparker, this morning, for the first time in my life, I just could not decide what to wear to the office! Something strange was holding me back from such a simple decision, and I knew I was going to be late for work. When I got out of the subway, I saw everyone looking up."

Howard said, "In many ways, things around me that were important before, seemed trivialized and irrelevant, but *not* the piano. The piano serves me as a place to go inward. I recalled hearing about the London blitzes during the Second World War, when Myra Hess gave concerts in the darkness while bombs were falling all around, and people listened and gained hope and strength. Yes, it is harder to focus and to work diligently at it, but it is important to turn to it and be enveloped by it for the comfort and solace it offers."

I recalled past instances when music had come to my rescue. For something as mundane as a forty-minute CAT scan, I "played" the forty-minute Brahms D Minor Piano Concerto in my head to block out the scary opticonscalometer machinery all around me and help the time to pass. I was so grateful for the wonderful resource of being able to enter a masterwork mentally, to hear it, let it imbue me, and get me through any thorny, adverse experience that confronts me.

Being enclosed in an MRI, as I had to be not long ago, was beyond adverse. A cheery technician had assured me that I could bring along a CD of my choice. So I selected Mozart—sublimely calming and uplifting Mozart—in this case, three piano concertos played by Alfred Brendel. From the moment I was conveyed through the narrow claustrophobic channel, eyes scrinched tightly closed lest I see where I actually was, it was clear that I would not hear one single note of the music. I was accosted by every cacophonous sound concocted by mankind: jackhammer drills, pneumatic pounding instruments, continual clanging, painful brain-bashing sounds beyond my threshold of tolerance.

I tried superimposing my Mozart, or Brahms, or Bach, in fits and starts, but all my usually reliable resources failed me this time. Instead I had to concentrate on not moving a muscle, not coughing, not letting tears burn through my lids to my eyes. I even tried to see the dark humor of their claim that the procedure was "uninvasive." I could not help wondering whether the molecules of my brain were being rearranged, or deranged? What price diagnostic reassurance? Sometimes music comes to my rescue and sometimes it doesn't.

With all the wisdom offered by my students and some professional musicians, neither the music, nor my own inner resources were pulling me out of the depression that overtook me on September 11. I did take comfort in my work; my students make me face surprising challenges each week; they are full of positive, loving energy, and I realize more and more what a creative force teaching is for me. It is among the great joys that compensate for the sorrows we have to endure. But my usual proprietary interest in the music they were studying, that makes me wish to play it as well, had all but disappeared. For the hours I was working with them, I was mercifully absorbed, but as soon as I was finished, the sense of all the evil and encroaching doom was overpowering.

For the first time in my life, I had no urge to play. I would come into the room and confront my piano head on: glare at it as it challenged me to approach, looming large and black, forbidding, unalluring somehow. Too available. Too potentially comforting. I wasn't ready or willing to be comforted. I consciously shunned my wonderful, dependable resource.

But then one day while driving in the car, I heard some beautiful piano music on the radio. It was in the key of G major, it was clearly Beethoven, and eventually, when the theme came around for the third or fourth time, I realized it was a rondo I had never heard. The pianist turned out to be Brendel, and I had an enormous response to it— the overwhelming sensation of wanting that piece for my very own. So when I got home, I tracked the piece down and sure enough, there it was: Rondo in G Major, Opus 51, No. 2, among some of my miscellaneous shorter Beethoven works. I spent the entire evening overdosing on it— playing it, devouring it obsessively, twenty, thirty times in a row. In many ways the piece seems like a tiny microcosm of the great G Major Piano Concerto. It was as though the little rondo had been sent to me, had risen up from the rubble like a phoenix, to rescue me from abandoning my beloved piano.

If the mere act of playing the piano, even striking a key and having the sound vaporize into thin air, can remind us of the ephemeral qualities of music, and indeed, of our own mortality, then conversely, the reiteration and constant refrain of a rondo theme can have the opposite message: that certain things are elemental and permanent. That reminder, along with the purity of the writing, seemed to have restored my spirit.

I programmed the extraordinary little rondo on all the recitals I was to give for the rest of the season. My rescue is just another debt of gratitude I owe to Beethoven.

My New York

IT doesn't matter how many times I cross the East River into Manhattan, I am thrilled at the majesty, the density, the energy, strength, and symbolism of the skyline, and all the life it contains. Its recent mutilation makes it all the more unbearably human. New Yorkers have a certain proprietary identification with and defensiveness about their city, which is lovable and friendly, no matter what anyone says.

When I was a young teenager, I took the train by myself to my piano lessons on the Upper West Side. I had no fears. I descended into the subway in Forest Hills, took the E train to Queens Plaza, changed trains, and got off at Columbus Circle, changing again for the train to the West Side, where I got off at West 72d Street. Coming up into the daylight, I crossed Broadway, avoiding the seedy types that hung around the little island park in the middle of the broad thoroughfare, and made my way to 171 West 72d Street, a *grande dame* of a building, where I studied with the *grande dame* Angela Weschler, from the New York College of Music, for two years. Each week I passed through the black iron gates of the building's inner courtyard and took the elevator up to her enormous apartment, where she greeted me with her special brand of Viennese hospitality.

None of the terrors or ills of the world known to my adult self now were in my youthful consciousness then. I was buoyed up by the New York spirit (as I still can be today), and I felt independent, jaunty, confident, alive. I was also blithely innocent, but I knew the city "ways" of a good girl: for example, you don't make eye contact while walking through the streets. But I saw everything. Every street, from the darkest, most commercial ones on the fringes of the city, lined with warehouses and double-parked trucks, to the most elegant shop-lined avenues, holds something of interest. In one *coup d'oeil* you may see an ancient Chinese woman, bent over and trudging along in silk slippers on the pavement, alongside a wealthy young society woman, straight blond hair swinging from side to side as one sheaf, clothed in couturier designs. She leaves a trail of perfume that costs $150 an ounce, and it fuses in your nostrils with the fumes from the homeless guy's urine-soaked trousers.

My fantasy for the past forty years has been to take the time to walk along every single street, both sides, from east to west, river to river, and back again, with a purseful of funds to indulge every whim—from swatches of great fabric and antique buttons obtainable in the garment district to frivolities displayed in the designer shops along Madison Avenue. I have had hundreds of good walks and browses over the years, although most of my days in New York City have been spent at work.

With all the childhood warnings about the wilds of Manhattan, I had to find out for myself that New York was the friendliest place: some of my best friendships began exactly there, and many a chance encounter with utter strangers yielded an entertaining tale. Once, in my favorite department store, Bergdorf Goodman, three of us were at the perfume counter shortly after opening time in the rush before Christmas—an elegant white-haired English gentleman paying $250 for a giant-sized bottle of something; a smart, sophisticated older woman; and me.

We were all waiting for the flustered salesgirl to finish the transaction with the gentleman when the older woman leaned over and said quietly to me, "There's the man to get to know!" I agreed it would be nice to get that gift package and asked her what sort of woman she thought he was buying it for.

"I imagine someone who looks something like you!" she ventured.

"Or you," I replied.

The saleslady disappeared for five minutes in search of a gift box and the three of us exchanged semi-amused glances.

"What scent have you purchased?" I asked the man.

"An ensemblay of Arpège," he answered proudly.

"He lost me," I whispered to the older woman. "Anyone who cannot pronounce 'ensemble' does not interest me."

"Honey, when you get to my age you'll realize that things like that don't matter. In fact, I think it's sort of endearing."

Then, turning to the man, she said with a twinkle in her eyes, "You realize you're making a shambles out of my marriage buying a gift like that."

"I'm trying to save my marriage from a shambles by buying it!" he replied with good humor.

He won me back. Finally in possession of his package, he bid us each happy holidays. The woman turned to me and asked, "What shall I buy myself? After thirty years of marriage my husband, while filling out insurance forms, asked me, 'What color are your eyes?'"

She bought herself some bath products, and I got my Annick Goutal *eau de parfum*. Three complete strangers, a typically friendly chance encounter in New York, at least in *my* New York.

I met my roguish good old Hungarian friend Rudi and his wife, Agi, on line backstage in the green room at Avery Fisher Hall, and I met the lovely Greek pianist Rita Bouboulidi in another green room at Carnegie Hall. For years Rita's abundantly positive and generous spirit enlivened her beautiful apartment in the ornate gothic building called Alwyn Court, on 58th Street, where she shared some mighty helpful pianistic tips during various visits over the years. Now she divides her time between New York and Europe.

On a freezing but fateful morning, at the corner of 61st and Madison, I was waiting with one other person for an uptown bus. She was an exceptionally attractive and chic older woman, and as we were both visibly chilled, we decided to share a taxi.

"How far up are you going?" she asked me.

"Eightieth Street." I was headed uptown to do an interview with the great jazz pianist George Shearing for *Clavier* magazine.

"Good. I am going to Seventy-ninth to the Acquavella Gallery."

"What is the exhibit?" I asked.

"A particularly fine postimpressionist show. You might enjoy it!"

As I had the time, we readily agreed that I would accompany her to the gallery before my interview. She was obviously of European background, a woman of high culture, and I was thrilled at the opportunity to share the exhibit and the animated conversation about concerts, music festivals, and musicians we knew in common. Subsequently we expressed the feeling that we had "made each other's day."

We exchanged telephone numbers, and she said, "Next time you are in the city let me know, and you will have lunch with me." Some weeks later, after several nice conversations, and despite lectures from our respective spouses that one should not "pick up strangers on the streets of Manhattan," I stepped off the elevator on the twenty-sixth floor of one of the most elegant New York residences, greeted warmly by my new friend, Andrea.

Upon entering her apartment I was confronted by one of my favorite Emil Nolde floral watercolors, hitherto known to me only in prints. Two more steps revealed her astounding aerie with spectacular city views and, more astoundingly, a mini-museum: a large Monet from his Thames series, a Bonnard bather, a Renoir pastel, Pissarro, Feininger, two Egon Schieles, sculptures by Lipschitz, Barlach, and Diego Giacometti, and so on and on.

Amused and delighted by my wonderment at seeing these great works in an intimate setting, she embraced me, visibly enjoying my pleasure, with not a trace of vanity or snobbism. During that first visit we shared some of our lives and feelings, and within a short time I also met her wonderful husband, Fred, with whom I coincidentally shared a birthday. Eventually we instituted a lovely ritual of joint dinner celebrations on that day, which still continues, with Fred very present but, alas, only in spirit. Andrea became one of my dearest friends and confidantes, seeing me through the end of one long mismarriage and attending my wedding to Ernest, with Freddie, who was already quite ill. To this day, twenty-five years after we met, we are still intimate friends.

My New York is Andrea, Rudi, Carnegie Hall, and its Recital Hall, where I felt like the queen of the city that day in February 1976 when I gave my debut recital. Also the Metropolitan Museum of Art (where Ernie sometimes mischievously gives me embarrassingly loud, smacking "museum kisses"), Steinway Hall, a variety of studios and hotel rooms wherein I enjoyed some memorable encounters with famous concert artists, and the Chelsea Antique Markets, which I visit occasionally with my daughter and her husband, who know every inch of the city. Not to mention a few favorite great restaurants.

In one legendary restaurant I celebrated and decompressed after my debut recital. The illustrious Russian Tea Room, "just a few steps to the left of Carnegie Hall" (as their advertisement boasted), closed in 2003, seventy-six years after it was opened by former members of the Imperial Russian Ballet. After the concert, a reception in the hall itself for the entire audience was hosted by my friends Phyllis and Marcia, and then, at about ten-thirty in the evening, a coterie of about twenty-five family and friends went next door to the Tea Room, where my parents had arranged a celebratory supper party. By then I didn't need any vodka, because I was fairly drunk with the excitement of the evening's events whirling around in my head, while still drawing from the adrenaline rush that began backstage before I went out to play.

The Russian Tea Room looked like Christmas all year long: reds above all, with green accents, gilded lighting fixtures, golden threads running through the red damask cloths, decorative samovars everywhere, illuminated paintings, chandeliers, and huge floral arrangements. The waiters wore Cossack costumes with brightly embroidered vests and sashes, and there was an air of festivity and celebration at every private tufted booth and table. We feasted on buttery blini, black and red caviar, borscht and sour cream, delicacies we revisited in the years to come. It was a unique spot, and I have heard rumors that it might reopen.

Other memorable restaurant experiences have included Hatsuhana, where André Watts first introduced me to exquisite Japanese delicacies (the start of my lifelong passion for Japanese cuisine), and Plaza España, a modest but excellent Spanish restaurant Ernest and I discovered many years ago.

But no culinary experience ever equaled our recent splurge at Nobu, downtown in Tribeca, where it is almost impossible to get a reservation. One day I got bitten by a zany bug or something. I dialed the restaurant and affected a snobbish voice—as though I had developed "Locust Valley lockjaw": "This is Carol Montparker. My husband and I are in town for one day only, and we would *so* like to visit Nobu's for lunch while we're here. Would it be possible to have a table?"

Perhaps the maître d' thought, from the authoritative tone of my voice, that he should have recognized my name. "Hold on, please."

We had passed round one: he hadn't hung up. One moment later: "We can give you a table at one-thirty. Will that be OK?"

We ordered the *omikase,* an eight-course chef's-choice menu, and each plate, each bite, was an exquisite sensual delight. Everyone should develop an affected upper-crust phone voice for just such purposes and pleasures.

These days I consider New York City from the outside, looking in. It isn't only the city's tragic victimhood and continuing vulnerability; we simply prefer to spend the occasional day, get injected with the energy, and then come home to the breezes on the porch, the smell of cut grass, and the gardens. Things change.

"Why Do You Keep Calling My Mother 'Dorothy'?"

STRANGE things started happening. For example, the day I invited Meg and Bob to a Sunday brunch, I scribbled the word "Meg" on the calendar for a month and a half later and promptly forgot about it. Our lives are so packed, especially when there are recitals coming up, that I just did not have room to keep it active in my brain.

We had bumped into each other at the Museum of Modern Art, and when I extended the invitation, I must have been feeling quite cavalier and gregarious, because the truth is that although Meg and I had been friends in college, we had not been in touch for years. Ernie and I like to entertain friends, we do it fairly often, and we do it well, I believe. But in this case, apparently, I was so preoccupied with practicing during every spare minute that the Sunday took on a heightened sense of preciousness; we generally give them away with great trepidation and care. What we really love to do on Sundays is nothing.

Which is exactly what we were doing that fine Sunday morning. In fact I was in old shorts and a T-shirt, and after practicing for a while for the concert, I got onto the treadmill with the news on TV; Ernie was busy upstairs. From my vantage point, I could see all the way down to the road, and I was mildly curious to know whose car had just turned into our long driveway. As it pulled up and alongside the window near the den where I was blithely treading along, my curiosity turned to abject panic as I realized whose car it was. I leapt off while it was still racing along. I've been told one can get a heart attack from that. A heart attack is what I was getting anyway, which seemed like a mercy and not a bad solution, considering I had to face and greet these nice folks who had made the trek to our house from Connecticut, starting early in the morning to arrive in time for Sunday brunch.

In the two minutes that it took for them to alight from their car, fetch their house gift from their trunk, and get to the front door, I suffered a momentary frisson of horror and self-flagellation at my irresponsible failure to scan the calendar before the weekend, which I had somehow assumed was free; then I quickly swung into action, hatching a plot, fluffing my hair (which seemed to have taken on a life of its own after standing up on end), plumping some pillows on the couch, and generally trying to straighten the entire part of the house that lay between my treadmill and the front door.

I couldn't bear telling them the truth. It was inexcusable to have forgotten a visit that apparently meant so much to the other couple. With what I consider to be great courage, I pulled the door open to reveal the face and body of a woman who in no way looked as though she expected company. I would have taken great pains to present myself as a person who has weathered the considerable number of years since college in admirably attractive shape. Instead, what they saw was a rather disheveled woman, caught in the throes of a physical fitness regime, looking like it wouldn't have helped at all anyway.

I said, or rather I spewed, all in one breath: "HI!!! I'm running a few minutes behind! I got so involved in practicing for my recital next week that I lost sight of the time! Actually I haven't felt too well this week, and I was almost going to call this all off, but I really wanted to see you, so I hope you'll forgive not only what I look like, but the fact that I didn't have the energy to put the house in the tip-top shape I would have loved to have you see it in, and so we decided that instead of making brunch, we're going to take you both out! HONEY, THEY'RE HERE!" This last I shouted in a hysterical tone to Ernie upstairs in the bathroom, praying that he would not yell back down, "Who the hell is 'they'?"

Already out of breath from my maniacal monologue, which I supposed proved that I am a pathological liar when I need to be, not that I'm too proud of that, I asked the stunned couple to make themselves comfortable on the porch and went to the refrigerator to see what, if any beverages besides wine vinegar and skim milk I could find therein. Nothing. So I swished a few teabags around in ice water, squeezed a lemon, threw a bit of sugar in, tossed in a sprig of mint from the garden, and presented my deluxe iced tea while I ran up to change.

On the way upstairs I hissed Ernie out of the bathroom, refreshed his memory as to who our guests were, suppressed an impulse to succumb to nervous lunatic cackling laughter at the acknowledgement of my hideous negligence. I told him to throw something decent on (his getup was even worse than mine—pajama bottoms with a dingy undershirt).

Now I am a person who spends, not a lot, but a *bit* of time thinking about what to wear for any given occasion. This occasion being a reunion with a college friend, under normal circumstances, I would have chosen something pretty, flattering to the figure, casual, but special in some way. My T-shirt and shorts were neither pretty nor flattering. In a crazed state, I flung my closet open, scooting outfit after outfit across the wooden dowel; it seemed as though I had absolutely nothing to wear in there that was appropriate or even possible. Mercifully, I calmed myself down sufficiently to be able to focus and grab a decent pair of slacks and a blouse, kick off my sneakers and slip into a pair of sandals, slather myself with deodorant and cologne, powder my nose, color my lips, brush my hair, and waltz onto the porch looking for all the world as though this was The Plan. Very shortly after, my poor abused husband moseyed in looking like a lost sheep (but a neat, obedient, and handsome lost sheep), somewhat dumbstruck at what was happening to his supposedly free Sunday.

Our guests seemed none the worse and fairly innocent of all the intrigue. We had some good conversation, and they asked me if I would play something from my recital program. I think I redeemed myself from whatever lapses they might have attributed to me. (Anyone who can play that music cannot be entirely senile.) One of the nicest things about being a pianist is that most of my friends seem to have unqualified respect for the hours of solitary work I have to do and are willing to excuse almost anything if it relates to the piano. I would not ordinarily exploit this knowledge, but at times like this, it is a useful asset. They are almost all great "customers" for pre-concert trial runs, and even if our guests had felt short-changed (which they miraculously had not), I knew that by giving a command performance, I might be able to charm even the surliest grouch out of a snit.

I am fairly certain that between the mini-concert and brunch at the best place in town, our friends felt happy and given to, but in the aftermath, even as I gained something in self-respect for whatever quick thinking I might have had in keeping my wits about me and salvaging the situation, I took note, not without a bit of concern, how being on overload was affecting me in unexpected, bizarre ways. Because that was not the only strange occurrence within a few days.

It certainly *was* a week when I was practicing my solo pieces in every cranny of time I could find. I was also rehearsing with the baritone for Schumann's *Dichterliebe* and ten Brahms songs. I was starting work on two other upcoming concerts and teaching my full complement of students, who have essentially made mincemeat of any schedule I might have started out with, by means of drivers' ed, sports, and other extracurricular events, sickness, and vacations. My calendar had so many crossed-out and rescheduled appointments scribbled in that it was hardly legible. I was also, incidentally, trying to rescue my husband and home from complete abandonment.

At various intervals, when I realized that I had not drawn a full deep breath in several hours, I went out for a walk, or to town for a browse. Life as a jigsaw puzzle is nothing new, but I was aware that the juggling act was getting more precarious. I even comforted myself with an almost mantralike quote from the great conductor Georg Solti (who was known to be an excellent pianist). When asked why he never gave piano recitals, his incredulous response was, "Are you kidding? To give a piano recital you have to drop everything else in your life and just practice!" Replaying that remark in my head always gives me (and, I suppose, anyone else who tries to do it all) succor and support.

My other lapse took place when, after practicing for three straight hours, I came up for air and noticed that time had crept up on me: I was expecting a student in just a few minutes. I began heating up a kettle to give a cup of tea and cookies to Mrs. Chiu, a lovely, generous woman and long-sacrificing mother, who drives her gifted son a great distance between his private school and his lesson. Relatively recently we had initiated addressing each other on a first-name basis, and so I invited Dorothy into my kitchen to watch the kettle and pour her own tea while Ryan and I began the lesson. Later on, I was reminding Dorothy to mark her calendar for an upcoming student workshop, and when I stopped speaking, Ryan interjected, "Why do you keep calling my mother 'Dorothy'?"

At that moment I realized that her name was Gloria, and that she had been delicate enough to respond unflinchingly to "Dorothy." With her tact and grace she probably would have responded to Hepsibah had I called her that. Where did I get Dorothy? Somewhere out of the aforementioned chaos of my life, I suppose, which is exactly how I explained myself to the now painfully blushing woman.

These stories can be told with humor but, in fact, there is obviously an insidious side to my life as it stands which is not at all funny.

One week before the aforementioned program, one of the most inspiring I have ever had the privilege of preparing and performing, Ernest said to me, "Norman recalled to me yesterday that many years ago he met you in the supermarket just before one of your concerts, and you told him emphatically, 'This is the very last concert I am ever performing.'"

I suppose anyone who knows me well would also recount their own experiences with similarly implied skepticism; I have obviously lost my credibility when I express, before every concert I have ever given, how I am most assuredly and adamantly convinced that it *will* be the very last. In fact, I have begun to notice merriment or amusement in the eyes of any to whom I might utter these extremely serious words. But it is nothing to laugh about, because it is agonizing to contemplate giving it all up; and it is also agony to continue.

Obviously I can no longer count upon the sympathy of others when I lament the tax performing publicly takes on my body, soul, and more recently, as noted, my mind! I have been in a constant struggle to eliminate those stresses from my life and enter a new phase. None of my loved ones wants me to see me suffering or distracted, so as they see it happening, they offer what seem like rational and acceptable alternatives. During the days just before a concert, I can absolutely foresee a happy future devoted to writing, gardening, homemaking, and teaching. I can envision the rest of my life essentially tension-free and organized, except for the odd snags fate throws. I could choose to say "Been there, done that," according to the advice one pianist-friend successfully adopted for herself in order to ease out of *her* torture.

Stories abound of world-renowned pianists who suffer the same agonies (Martha Argerich, André Watts, Peter Serkin, and Peter Frankel, all good company); misery *loves* company, but in the end it doesn't help. In reality, it is probably the most difficult profession from which to retire: if you *can* do it, you feel you *must* do it. The ability to do it is an entity unto itself, and it wants to be expressed. Doing it, playing, performing music one loves is as joyful as it is taxing. Being a pianist is what I am and do. I would mourn the loss of that identity.

The night before this particular concert, I awoke with a feeling of dread before I even remembered what day was dawning. The bilious sensation in my gut is one that I have learned to snidely welcome with a wry "Oh, hello, nerves, what took you so long?" but in reality it is a rotten feeling, and I would like never to feel it again. Who knows what that does to one's innards? I was able to assuage the nerves with a combination of homeopathic remedies and Xanax, but by the time I got backstage, in spite of the best intentions, yoga exercises, deep breathing, and any other device I could drum up, I was trembling with fright and anticipation. I was flushed and could feel that my blood pressure was quite elevated. My immune system, weakened by a tour in the hospital a month earlier, wasn't helping. This was no longer a question of "should I or shouldn't I?" This was becoming a question of survival. Just the day before, one of my adult students related a charming anecdote about a female concert pianist who had recently dropped dead in the middle of her concert. I did not find it amusing. That could be me. Another friend phoned to say she had given up a love affair because it was causing more pain than joy. It takes courage to give up something you love so much. Amidst all the dark thoughts, occasional windows opened up through which I could see what I am supposed to see: the prospect of giving joy to others through my music. After all, I have chosen to play because I love it.

The concert went extremely well. I am used to this: whatever disasters I anticipate might befall me in concert never do. I got over my initial nervousness, felt inspired, and from the response of a full house and from my own point of view, which is, of course, the only one I truly care about, I was almost entirely pleased, and grateful for my stamina to handle all those notes per square inch of page of music by this genius, Mendelssohn, the ecstatic, whose music is boundlessly energetic.

Almost a week after the concert, and I was in mourning. Before the concert, when I was suffering from nerves, I had sworn on things I hold holy that I would cease to accept invitations to perform solo anymore, and I am superstitious enough to know that once having sworn, I would keep to it. If the New York Philharmonic called and asked me to step in to play the Brahms First Piano Concerto or the Schumann or a Beethoven, would I be able to resist? Well, they didn't call, of course, so I had no dilemma.

But there did come an invitation, one week later, to play the Bach D Minor Clavier Concerto with a chamber orchestra, an opportunity that does not grow on trees. Would this gig constitute a "solo performance?" *No,* I began to rationalize. There are very few solo passages without at least the basso continuo accompaniment. What about the fact that I had two other previously scheduled programs within the same month to practice?

Every fool who is also a pianist knows that the pain of solo performance is not unlike labor pains, quite quickly forgotten in the flush of possibility, accomplishment, and success.

I actually had the courage to decline the invitation—at first. I heard myself uttering words I did not think were in my musical vocabulary: "NO, thank you." Then everything conspired against my resolve. I heard a beautiful Andras Schiff performance of the very same work the next day on the radio, and I received the wonderful Murray Perahia CDs of all the Bach keyboard concertos in the mail that very same day: a mysterious case of synchronicity, in New Age jargon, and there are those who believe that there are no coincidences—that everything is meant as a lesson. I made the mistake of taking the music out and playing it, and Ernie shouted in from the next room, "Wow, Carol! That's beautiful! What is it?"

That did it.

I telephoned the artistic director who had called to invite me, asking whether I had missed the boat—was the invitation still open?

"Yes, I am very glad you decided to do it," she replied.

Ryan's Awakening

THE room looked inviting and ready, but I went around arranging pillows, dusting the two black pianos (which *always* seem to need dusting), turning lamps on for ambience, adding some extra chairs, and just enjoying the pleasure of anticipation. In a half hour, my twelve students would arrive for a playing class, a regular feature of my teaching every several months. I have enjoyed my teaching over the course of the past thirty years, but at this moment I realized that I was excited by it. The same core of students had been with me for a while, seen and heard each other's progress, even seemed to care about each other—a particularly nice, uncompetitive, generous group, and all of them excited by the piano.

This evening I realized I was particularly anxious for them all to witness fourteen-year-old Ryan's metamorphosis from a talented student to a young artist during the period since the last class. Nothing is as thrilling to me as that instant. With most students there is a gradual process of maturation. Layers of technical facility, understanding, expressiveness, and experience are piled on, and eventually the results pay off. But with a few rare others, I get to witness the moment when it all clicks, as it did with Ryan.

I had inherited Ryan five years earlier from Charlotte, another one of my students, a fine teacher of younger piano pupils. It was a generous gift she gave to me, but we both acknowledged that as bright and musical as he was, he was a slacker, and not particularly interested in practicing. But one day he announced at a lesson, "I want to enter a competition."

It shocked me, but I said, "You'll have to do some fancy practicing if you want that, Ryan, because you are simply not ready yet. You have the musicality and intelligence, but you have not learned how to work."

He looked at me, committing to nothing, but with apparent understanding, and I had no way of knowing what to expect. Until then he had managed to weasel through his lessons with minimal preparation, and we had had historic "issues" over his failure to read the little spiral notebook into which I scribble weekly assignments and key points that need attention. He was an honors student and had recently been accepted to an excellent private high school (with the nickname "the pressure cooker") that requires from him a considerable commute, leaving no time for much else. Prior to switching schools, he preferred to indulge his free time with any diversion other than hard study, having learned that his keen intellect would let him sail through most challenges more than creditably well.

I never raise my voice nor express anger to my students. I find that a quiet expression of my disappointment goes much further, and so I confronted Ryan.

"You know what I think? I think you are so used to being told how bright you are, which, of course, you are, that you are convinced you can get by in everything you do on brains alone. Well, I have news for you: it won't work on the piano. Your fingers do not have brains in them. They have muscles that need to be *guided by* your brains, and they need development, and that's called 'practicing.' It's never going to happen unless you are willing to work. I think you are a very nice person, and I enjoy teaching you, but I am disappointed with your unwillingness to work and nourish your talent."

The next lesson revealed that my stern lecture had paid off. He had found a good practice piano at school and was better prepared than I had hoped. I rolled up my sleeves and dug in.

My challenge, as ever with young talents, is to try to hasten along their understanding and perceptions of huge concepts like taste, discernment, and "feelings" commensurate with an emotional and psychological maturation they simply do not yet have. I play; I try to explain what it means to sing a long Chopin melodic line in bel canto style; I try to inject the sound of ego into their egoless young psyches; I try to coax the *largesse* past their fingers into their arms and from there into their bodies, and thence into their whole selves; I demonstrate and then convert into the relative poverty of words what the grandiose opening chords of a polonaise require from their spirit, and likewise the bittersweetness of the ensuing bars, laden with the peculiar variety of Polish melancholy called *zäl*; I give a mini-lesson in Polish and Russian history, quoting someone's apt description of Chopin's polonaises as "guns wrapped in roses."

And lo! My hair stands on end as Ryan responds, and I turn to his mother, quietly reading her Chinese newspaper, but with her ear to her gifted son's performance, and I exclaim, "Did you hear that? That was Ryan, not me!" And we both stifle tears as witnesses to an important event. Then Ryan, seeing he has effected such a deep response, realizes that he has opened a magic door. He perceives his power to move. And he is thus initiated.

I sit down at the keyboard and demonstrate rubato, the literal "robbing" of time and the giving back, so essential to the music.

"Music is *of* us. It breathes, it is not robotic and rigid. You must hold back on the most deeply expressive places, then make it up by pressing urgently forward." I stop short of spoon-feeding him which spots are the most expressive ones. Ryan gets it, takes to the concepts naturally.

I press his hand deeper into the keybed; I softly rotate his hand from the wrist, to ensure the relaxation of his playing; I take his fingers into my hand and massage the fleshy pads, telling him, "This is the part of your fingers that will produce the most sensuous tone. You must sensitize your pads to the extent that you can actually feel the 'buzz,' the vibrations of the strings through the piano directly into your fingers. Then you will want to experience that extra dimension of pleasurable response in your hand and your sound each time you sit at the instrument."

He is too young to truly know what "sensuous" means, but somehow he does what I ask. I flush with excitement for what is happening in front of my eyes and ears. He has two weeks to prepare a tape of this Chopin Polonaise in C-sharp Minor for acceptance in a master class. We put aside his Haydn sonata and Poulenc pieces, and I tell him to work exclusively on the Chopin.

The following week he sits down and puts his adolescent hands on the keys, and out come the opening octaves with startling command and authority. I am riveted. Ryan is not chatty. It isn't always easy for me to know what he is thinking. I only know he *is* thinking. Now I knew he was also hearing, fully. I look at him and I no longer see the child who came to me, with his shock of beautiful black hair and plump young physique. I realize that here, now, is a young man, lean, tall, with large hands that now reach a ninth handily. Not only is he is proving that he heard and absorbed every instruction, but he is *doing* it all, not copying, but experiencing it.

I cannot know what he will plan to do with what he has just discovered, where he will go with it. Anything he decides will be

OK. Essentially my biggest job is accomplished, although luckily I will have him for three more precious years, through high school. I got him over the hump and held his hand as he crossed the big bridge, so that he can now see the light of what there is for him in music's vast store. The rest is relatively easy, and I am along for the joyride.

Break a Leg!

"BREAK a leg" (and "Hals und Bein bruck!" [break neck and bone!], the version of one of my teachers) are words disallowed to any of my well-wishers before a concert, as all who know me are well aware. (Actually, I think the best wish for a performing artist is "Enjoy your concert.")

I always thought it was one broken leg per customer, but twice in my life, sixteen years apart, I had the auspicious occasion to break my leg or my foot. In both cases, I have to admit, I was rushing around wearing sandals that offered dubious support. The memory of the terror and the tremendous inconvenience was apparently never sufficient enough to slow me down. Only the infirmity itself slowed me down, as noted by certain folks who see me as "overactive"; they told me they had never seen me "so peaceful, so passive." (I guess I'll be even more peaceful and passive when I'm dead!)

The only scant recompense of such disasters is in the recounting of the tale, and then the enforced quiet time to think and write. In the first event, while rushing down the basement stairs, I came out of my sandal and went over the side of the staircase, which in those days had no banister. I was alone in the locked-up house except for Polly, my beloved dog, who, only this once, disappointed me by keeping her distance, out of fear, instead of bringing me a keg of beer or something comforting as rescue dogs are meant to do. I could have quietly expired if my father had not earlier installed an illegal phone extension in the basement, to which I dragged my broken body to call for help.

A friend broke into the house, gave me some aspirin until my husband arrived, and called the ambulance. I suffered multiple fractures, including the tibia, broken clean across because of the freakish way my leg had bent sideways over the stairs, and I required a full-length cast for six excruciating months after a long hospital stay.

It was one of the worst traumas of my life, but to paraphrase a great philosopher, "That which does not kill you, strengthens you." It jogs one's appreciation for folks who have that daily struggle all their lives, it begets ingenuity in trying to alleviate the pain and frustration, and it is a challenging exercise in positive thinking in the face of adversity. In that spirit, halfway through the siege, I imagined and ultimately presented an elegant *soirée musicale* for my friends, including my orthopedic surgeon and his wife. I practiced and baked and carried it off, except for the omission of the left pedal (a feat [*foot?*] in itself), while hiding my ugly white cast under a beautiful black velvet skirt. I had thrown my walker into the car and driven myself to my favorite clothing store (actually, my car knows how to get there without me), and I hobbled my way around until I found the lovely garment, such was my determination.

At the end of six months I had a crazy quilt of imagery and vignettes, one decent leg, and another slightly crooked one. Among the sketchy reminiscences was one so-called consulting orthopedic surgeon who showed up at my hospital bedside and, knowing I was a pianist, proceeded to extract from his overstuffed wallet an array of concert tickets, which he fanned out like a full hand of cards. His pompous and boastful display, as though the number of concert tickets were the measure of the cultured man, rather disgusted me, especially as he never gave a glance at my leg! A month later we received an astronomical bill (I should have billed *him* for having to abide his conceit) for his consulting "services" that my husband and I decided forthwith to ignore. After receiving several warnings, I phoned his office to ask that they forward the bill to our insurance carriers and was informed by his formidable wife, the office manager, that their office did not accept insurance. A few more dire threats from dunning agencies prompted me to write the following personal letter, addressed to the pretentious physician himself:

> Dear Dr. ——,
> I was ever so grateful to have my hospital pain and boredom relieved by your visit to my bedside at Huntington Hospital, especially the chance to speak about music, and take my mind off my misery with a connoisseur such as yourself.
>
> By the way, there seems to be a misunderstanding with your office and the billing department. We can only afford to pay your fee through insurance. Would you kindly intervene and forward our bill to the proper channels?

We never got another bill. The flattery to his ego was exactly what was needed.

The second time I "only" broke my foot, a trauma only for the first four days in a cast, or rather, a mis-cast, put on by the emergency room doctors. Using a walker or crutches put such a strain on my poor hands and pectoral and arm muscles that I felt I was heading for a train wreck, never again to play the piano without pain. Once I visited my orthopedic specialist, however, he angrily cut off the cast, threw it across his examining room, mumbling something about the incompetence of the doctor who had fashioned the contrivance, and placed a heavenly, albeit in no way fashionable, boot on my foot that enabled me to take little light steps until it healed. For the time being, however, both the damper pedal and the car's gas pedal were off limits.

I think the pedaling challenges during those off months were helpful exercises. Doing without the *una corda* pedal, without an active left foot, enhanced my ability to effect tonal nuances without reducing the number of strings; going without the damper pedal is a spur to developing the best legato and sostenuto you can, with only your bare hands for tools. I wouldn't recommend that a pianist go to those extremes to develop any of these skills, but I did have an elucidating conversation with Radu Lupu a year after I had coped with my broken leg, and it so happened that he, too, having somehow mysteriously "jumped through the floor like Rumpelstilskin," as he described it, had to play a concert with a cast, and without the *una corda* pedal.

In my case, the problem is living in haste. I had been hustling, as is my wont, this time to the post office to mail a gift to a friend. It's like they say: no good deed goes unpunished. I do not think I can change my ways—neither my metabolism nor my voracious compulsion to stuff as much into life as I can. I *would* like to experience what it would be like to be a lady of leisure, before it is all over, but I doubt I ever will.

A Mother's Sacrifice

"MY name is Natasha Petrov. You will teach me?" The high-pitched voice on the phone was timid, and the Eastern European–inflected English, faltering. The young woman's plea from the heart pierced all my resolve to resist accepting any new students; I was teaching more than I wanted to already and needed more time to study new literature during the hiatus I had taken from solo performance. But I have no defenses, it seems, against attractive invitations to play and intriguing calls such as these. She had been given my number by a friend who told me that she sounded so earnest and serious about her piano study, he was certain I would want to meet her.

"Can you come to my home and let me hear you play?"

"Yes, I will pass the phone to my mother."

The mother's English was just adequate to understand my directions, but she managed to inform me, during our short conversation, of their joint dream of a piano career for her daughter and an education at the Juilliard School. Would I prepare her for the entrance exam?

"Let me hear her play, and we will see what happens."

I don't know what I expected to hear. Knowing the excellence of many European conservatories and sensing a devotion to her

220

dream, I entertained the notion that it would be a relatively short project for us to achieve her goal. I anticipated language difficulties, but I have dealt with that before. I use my hands a lot, Italian style, to enhance my speech, and I always resort to demonstration at the keyboard, with the assumption that music, the so-called universal language, would get me through any difficulty.

At the precise moment of our appointed meeting, my doorbell rang, and I greeted two attractive blond-haired women: the older was tall, well-coiffed, elegantly dressed in a business suit, a silk blouse, high heels, and a string of pearls; the younger, who looked about sixteen, was, in fact, twenty—quite pretty, but with a pallid complexion, petite, and very shy, almost hiding behind the mother.

Once inside, they looked around at my room with a wide-eyed Alice-in-Wonderland curiosity that was both touching and embarrassing. The mother, Olga, burst forth with a monologue revealing her passionately focused ambitions for the girl.

"Her father was a musician and died when she was very small. I have her music still in Europe, and I will send for it. She practiced very hard for you, and we brought the book from Juilliard. Show her, Natasha."

The girl stepped forward and showed me the conservatory catalog, turning right to the page of requirements.

"What did you bring to play for me today?"

"Bach?" she asked me in return.

"Very good. Please don't be nervous. Here. Sit at this piano, and begin whenever you want." The poor girl was shaking violently. She began to play a little prelude from an intermediate-level book of short works by Bach, a long way from the preludes and fugues from the formidable *Well-Tempered Clavier* required for the admissions. She played the notes cleanly, but with the most unconventional and random fingering I ever saw, not a flutter of pedal, and a touch that barely grazed the keys. In one minute I recognized the pipe dream that these two women, mother and daughter, were living. From this first small sampling, it seemed clear to me that there was a slim chance she would be accepted by the illustrious institution, this year or possibly ever.

Two pairs of blue eyes were riveted onto me for my reaction after Natasha finished the Bach piece, and I felt myself in a deep dilemma. Such hope and expectation all over their faces, and I had to be certain that my own did not reflect my deep concern and predicament. With what I hoped was a cheery smile, I told Natasha that she had played the Bach very well. I am certain that my tiny bit of encouragement was interpreted, by both of them, to mean that their dream had practically come true, so I hastened to add, "You will have to work very, very hard and possibly for several years before you will be ready for that audition. Are you willing to work very hard?"

"Yes!" Such an eager "yes"! And I have witnessed near-miracles occur, born of intense motivation, desire, hard work, and concentration. Here I was with yet another major challenge in my own life, after just a ten-minute meeting. Did I need another huge challenge? No. Was she irresistible? Yes.

On the plus side, she was obviously somewhat musical. She knew how to phrase in a natural way, although the music was quite indulgently out of rhythm. She had lots of time to practice and the love and willingness to give herself over to it. Her scales and arpeggios were fluent, confident, and strong. Good. That was one small facet of the requirements we would not have to deal with.

She had never studied a Beethoven sonata. One glance at the catalog indicated that any opus she might have been able to handle technically had been ruled out by the conservatory. Choosing one would be difficult, but teaching it, an arduous journey. Any Beethoven sonata is a journey, but teaching a girl who nods as though she understands what you have said even if she quite possibly has not would be a journey across the roughest terrain. Feeling reckless and against all my teaching philosophies and wisdom, I asked her if she owned the Beethoven sonatas.

"Yes, in Europe," the mother answered.

"We need them right now. I will lend you my extra copy, but you will have to buy your own or copy pages from mine, because we have to get to work immediately."

She played me a Chopin nocturne that she wanted to complete, and it was an utter mess: inaccurate bass notes, no pulse, and worst of all, not a single cantabile tone in the entire piece. But as soon as I played some phrases and placed my fingers on her arm, demonstrating the pressure and depth of touch I wanted her to apply into the keybed, she began to get it. I think she was surprised at the intimacy of my gesture, of my kneading her bare arm, but I have transgressed the morés of more formal cultures than hers, by touching and holding the arms, hands, and fingers of Asian students whose families don't even hug each other. I didn't have the time to wait for a long-term closeness to develop; I was overwhelmed by a sense of no-nonsense and no time to waste when it came to this twenty-year-old. It would not be easy, but I had, much to my amazement, in the short meeting, already developed an empathy and interest in this sweet young person, who seemed so lost.

I wrote down the names of the books of music that I wanted her to buy before the next lesson, and her mother stepped in again.

"Please, Ms. Montparker, here is my credit card. You call and order for us? They will not understand me on the phone."

The name on the credit card was an unpronounceable conglomeration of consonants, not at all Eastern European, but rather Southeast Asian. I must have looked perplexed, because the older woman, who really owed me nothing in the way of explanations, felt the need to say, "You see, I came here few years ago, and I met a man, and he was willing to marry me, so that I could send for my daughter."

I called Patelson's Music House, ordered the music, and arranged our lesson time. Another piece of my precious personal life was disappearing before my eyes, not that I hadn't been entirely responsible for my decision, as I reminded myself while the transaction took place. But when I meet someone with such fervor and pure love of the piano, like this young woman clearly had (despite, and not because of, her mother's ambitions for her), my own love for the instrument and for imparting that love to others comes flooding in, leaving me completely disarmed.

As the two were leaving, I noticed a car and driver facing away from my house, ready to drive down to the road.

"That is my husband," Olga explained.

I walked over to the car to meet him. Two fierce German shepherds nearly leapt out of the window at me.

I asked, "Are they bad dogs?"

"If they know you won't hurt me, they'll calm down. When she first came," he pointed at Natasha and laughed, "they almost ate her."

I hardly knew this man. Perhaps he had some redeeming qualities, but I can only hope that I again succeeded in masking my first impressions. During our short exchange, I could discern no single characteristic that would have brought the two together in marriage. They seemed so different. She was fair, tall, attractive, assertive, and upbeat; he was slight, swarthy, and scowling.

The three drove off together leaving me with a hundred possible scenarios about how they got together spinning around in my head. What I kept concluding was that some sort of desperation might lead a mother to acts of great heroism, courage, and sacrifice.

The following week Natasha came with her new music and a wad of cash, which she handed me saying, "Is for ten lessons."

(Was that the time they expected me to accomplish her preparation for the audition?) In the hour and a half that followed, I experienced a mix of hope and frustration as I kept discovering gaping loopholes in her questionable course of study in her country. I used the piano and plenty of sign language to get my points across. She nodded and answered "Of course" each time I asked her if she understood, but I kept wondering how much she truly did. I could only hope that as the weeks went by, however many I would be granted, more and more would sink in. She was studying English at a local high school.

After two weeks I doubted she would ever get into Juilliard; after three weeks the probability shifted slightly in a positive direction. She had some problems in the rhythm department and was unused to following notated fingering; she also had other miscellaneous bad habits that made me think she was largely an autodidact. She had the disconcerting habit of using her own dynamic impulses instead of the composer's notated ones. If she felt a certain passage should swell with emotion, why, then, she played a crescendo leading to a *fortissimo,* when the music indicated only *piano.* I scolded her for her indulgences and tried to instill a sense of responsibility to the written score as gospel; but only when I suggested that the judges at an audition would penalize her for playing the wrong dynamics did she take it seriously.

However, in spite of these struggles, I began to detect changes: she started to employ a deeper touch and follow the notations more accurately. At eight weeks I secretly marveled at both her and myself. I told her how excellent her Bach prelude and fugue were, and how much progress she had made in the Sonata, Opus 1, No. 1, by Beethoven. (I still had serious concerns about her Chopin, with her limitations in playing legato or cantabile, but I did not express those.) It was the first time I allowed myself to give her a measure of hope, and it unstoppered a dam between us. Tears came to her eyes, and she pulled her fist down in the triumphant gesture that athletes make when they score: *yes!*

I allowed Natasha to perform her Bach prelude and fugue in her first informal recital with my class of students in my home. My other students usually dress too informally for my taste, but Natasha arrived in a strapless gown. I felt her embarrassment for having overdressed, evidence of her excitement and overzealousness. But I was utterly fascinated to watch her perform for the first time with the sudden appearance of inappropriately emotive body gestures that bordered on exhibitionistic, as though she had copied them from a cheap movie with some grade-C actress imitating her idea of a concert artist. At the next lesson I had the difficult task of delicately explaining to her how those affectations were neither attractive nor necessary nor beneficial to her technique. I sat myself down and exaggerated her exaggerations. My parody made her blush profusely, but then I managed to cajole her into seeing the humor, and she could finally laugh with me. Another hurdle was cleared.

Even though Natasha had misjudged the recital attire, it was obvious that she and her mother had style. I know many European women who seem to know intuitively how to put themselves together. Natasha came to her lessons smartly dressed, and after her impressive advance payment at the outset, I felt I could at least assuage my concerns that the lessons would be a financial struggle for them as recent immigrants.

So I was entirely unprepared when my friend related the circumstances under which he had met Olga: he was visiting at the home of a wealthy family where she was working as their home nursing aide. Then he described the small apartment over a warehouse alongside railroad tracks, with its three unlikely cohabitants and Natasha's tiny spinet.

I phoned around and persuaded a public library and a local

piano shop to agree to allow Natasha to practice for several hours each week on their good pianos. These arrangements lasted only a short while, alas, and Natasha was back on her spinet. Trying to develop even a vague concept of good tone on such an orange-crate of an instrument is a definite disadvantage.

In the weeks that followed, certain discouraging lapses in communication set us back. I noticed Natasha wince and bristle any time I marked the old Chopin edition from which she was studying a ballade.

"Here, please to mark the copy instead," she pleaded.

"Will you be practicing from the copy or the book?"

"The book."

"Well," I said quite firmly, "I want you to practice from whichever music I mark. You must *see* the corrections daily. If I mark the copy, then practice from the copy; or else I will mark the book. You understand?"

"Of course. But you see, is old music. It was my father's."

A small window of understanding had opened up. Her father had been a musician, but she had never known him. Obviously that accounted for her strong ties to the music and her boundless motivation.

I ventured, "Perhaps your father would have been happy to know that his daughter was using his music."

Her face tensed, her expression darkened, and she made a gesture that dismissed my conjecture, with the clear message that I had stepped too far beyond her boundaries of privacy. I apologized and told her I would only mark her photocopies. The following week she countered by insisting that I mark the book itself, but only with a pencil. Yet another obstacle overcome.

The role of a teacher in a one-on-one dynamic is as diverse as human nature itself. Some piano students have to be discouraged from unburdening themselves throughout the entire lesson, as though the piano teacher were a psychologist. One adult student even confessed to me, "You're cheaper than a shrink!" In every case, certain personal and privileged information is revealed that both solidifies the relationship, and casts light on the character and potentialities of the student.

With Natasha I had to step lightly. She had difficulties with comprehension, and I could not determine whether the problem stemmed from intellect or language skills. I was completely at sea. On one occasion I demonstrated a passage at least a dozen times, faster and lighter than she was playing it. I used every descriptive: metaphor and analogy, musical Italian, English, sign language. I drew pictures, from feathers to butterflies, but I couldn't get her to grasp the concept of the leggiero passage; and the problem was not a lack of technique. In the end, I let it go, shrugging to myself and acknowledging that I had given it my best shot, using more energy than I knew I had.

Natasha also had a fragile ego from her difficult past, and ego is an essential element for success as an artist. We had to develop at least the *sound* of ego in her playing, so I encouraged her to emulate my sound whenever she could, which is not my ideal modus operandi.

While Natasha's ego was fragile about certain things, she was surprisingly aggressive in other ways. One day she walked in and announced that it was her birthday.

"That's nice," I said. "I would like to give you a little something."

Immediately she offered, "Maybe you give me some free lessons." My jaw must have dropped open, as I was already giving her much more than the hour she was paying for.

I replied, "No, Natasha, I cannot do that, but here is a nice CD of some Chopin." She accepted it with a mumbled "Thanks" and a little shrug.

On several occasions Olga asked me with intense anxiety, right in front of Natasha, "Tell me, how is she doing?"

Her emotional urgency frightened me, especially with its overtones of ambitiousness.

I replied, "She is working very hard, and she is doing very well so far, but it will take a lot of time and patience. You understand?" I looked directly into her concerned blue eyes—I seemed to be seeing into her soul—and I am not certain she enjoyed my response, but after a few minutes she spontaneously embraced me, thanking me for the work I was doing with her daughter.

One afternoon during her lesson, I tried to suggest other possibilities.

"Natasha, I think it would be a good idea if you would apply to more than one school, in case you do not get admitted to Juilliard."

She replied, "I only want to go to Juilliard."

"Yes, I understand, Natasha, and perhaps you will get in, but perhaps you will not! There are no guarantees! Many gifted musicians want to go there too. They have this much room"—I put my hands about a foot apart—"but this many musicians want to go there"—I spread my arms out wide. "What will you do if you do not get in? Spend your days in your apartment practicing on your little piano? Wouldn't it be better to have an alternate choice so that at least you would be in a school? Juilliard is not the only fine school, you know. Then, if you wanted to, you could try to transfer." The reality was that the level of applicants for every conservatory was at record highs, and I did not believe she could handle the intellectual requirements at a university with a good music department.

After all my energy, trying to articulate what I felt to be a very important issue with far-ranging danger, Natasha looked at me with a blank robotic stare and repeated her mantra, her mother's dream as much as hers: " I only want to go to Juilliard."

I shuddered to think of the sacrifices, the dreams, the disappointments, my unwitting role in (and indeed increasingly central to) their ambitions, and the task that was before me. I could only determine to teach her as well as I could so that she would end up playing better than either she or I could predict, but the uncertainty of her future was undeniably weighing upon me greatly, so much so that I found I was angry and annoyed at myself for assuming this burden in the first place.

My salvation came the following week when Natasha walked in visibly upset. Without looking me in the eye, she blurted out, "My mother asked that you call and find me someone from Juilliard to teach me before the audition."

Ordinarily, the audacity of such a brazen request would have affronted and shocked me, but instead, I experienced a powerful phenomenon: a spontaneous rush of relief, almost like the gushing of an open valve in my head.

"Of course," I replied, and forthwith dialed the fabled conservatory's office of career management, where they have a roster of names of alumni and faculty who teach privately. I requested the list be sent to Natasha's home address straightaway. Gladly would I defer, relinquish, and bequeath the burden to the next unwitting teacher.

I knew that no student had ever been given more energy, patience, or indulgence, nor made as much progress in as short a time, against greater odds. I wish her at least a piece of her dream.

Copying Calder

WHEN my ninety-year-old father was a mere whippersnapper of eighty, during a visit to our house he chanced to notice an art book on Alexander Calder lying on our coffee table. He flipped through the pages as I watched his face, more perplexed than amused. I wanted so much for him to appreciate and understand the way that Calder took his sense of humor and construed it into serious art that has delighted my husband and me, among many other millions of people. I will never forget the unbridled laughter coming out of each gallery of a Calder show we attended at the Cooper-Hewitt Museum in New York. Indeed, every Calder show is crowded with families; long ago I took my kids to the Whitney Museum lobby to watch his famous animated *Circus*, created out of wire, corks, straw, buttons, and all sorts of questionable and ephemeral materials not so easily distinguishable.

"This crazy stuff is in *museums?*" My father was dumbfounded. He added, "Who couldn't make this?"

The fact is that Calder and my father had several important traits in common, whether my father knew it or not. They both had a sweet sense of humor, both could draw fairly well, and both practically walked around with a pair of pliers in their pockets. There is nothing that my father, a retired wholesale hardware salesman, couldn't fix; no matter how confounding the problem, his ingenuity figured out how to make it run again. Among the bushels of grommets, nuts, and bolts that surrounded him in his downtown store were reels upon reels of every kind of wire known to man. Calder used to say he "thought best in wire," referring to his three-dimensional contoured-wire sculptures: caricatures of friends, animals, circus performers, jewelry, anything. Those articulate and ingenious pieces are uncanny and, in my mind, inimitable, but I called my father's bluff and challenged him by bringing him a pair of pliers and a few wire coat hangers from my closet.

For the next few hours, my father, who is rather garrulous, said not a word other than to command me "Go take a walk!" when I approached the sofa to see what he was up to. By the time he came up for air, he had produced several animals in the style of Calder—naive, elemental, graceful, and certainly amusing. The pig and the cow that he fashioned that day are still on my fireplace mantel, delighting all visitors, including my dear friend Andrea, a serious art collector who commissioned my father to create one for her.

"Where will you put it?" I asked her, picturing my father's little offering against the backdrop of her elegant apartment, its walls covered with impressionist and postimpressionist paintings, complemented by her collection of beautiful sculptures.

"On the sideboard under the Monet," she replied, without batting an eye.

"What will you say when anyone asks you whose it is?"

"I will reply, 'Oh you know,' and let them wonder!" she answered with mischievous glee.

And so it has gone with my father's Calder copies. When my grandson Rollie was one year old, he pointed to one of the wire sculptures on the mantle and blurted out one of his first words: "Pig!" he said, triumphantly and most assuredly.

Dad's preoccupation with spools of wire and pliers lasted only a few weeks, whereupon he went on strike, flatly refusing to take any more orders, in spite of the fact that one of my cousins was certain he could interest a gallery owner in carrying these neo-Calderesque creations.

For me, the great charm of Calder's work, particularly the wire figures and the hanging mobiles, is how they dispense with mass and float in space. Much of his work is abstract, but his themes often represent plant and animal life, moving gracefully when touched or caught in a draft of air; in one museum catalog, they were likened to "the leaves of a tree, a flock of birds or a school of fish."

I have been absolutely haunted by Calder's extraordinary mobile of a fish ever since my husband and I saw it hanging in the Peggy Guggenheim collection in Venice some years ago. The skeleton was fashioned from wire, and the scales were bits of multicolored glass, each of which dangled independently, catching and refracting the light as it swung in space. Then, some years later, while visiting the National Gallery in Washington, D.C., we saw several other examples of his glass and wire fish mobiles, not quite as vivid as the Venetian example, but also mesmerizing.

One day, after I had completed a series of concerts, I was confronted with a strange sensation that I could not quite identify. It definitely was a rare and really good feeling, and I finally recognized it as leisure! But it also felt weirdly uncomfortable, and I couldn't decide how to "utilize" it. I should have stared into space, a pastime I find enormously attractive but have almost lost the knack of: my brain races into high gear and I imagine all sorts of new projects. It was in such a suspended state that I came up with the idea of crafting two fishes.

I have been collecting beach glass for years: the smoothness of the edges, the mellowed opacity of the colors, the prismatic glow of glass as a medium have long delighted me. But accumulating there in a big bowl, all these shards of every shape and size, mostly in shades of bottle green, seemed to be crying out to be fashioned into fish. I have a strong belief that if a person stares long and hard enough at a problem, the solutions will emerge. Contemplating photos of the Calder masterpieces, I noted that some of his dangling glass bits were perforated with little holes through which the wire was threaded, but others had been wrapped in wire. I had plenty of spools of strong, fine wire, and I am not a person who gives up easily once I get a notion; so what if jewelers and glaziers were telling me that to pierce a hole in a piece of glass requires a diamond head drill, and costs an average of five to ten dollars per hole, without guarantees that the glass won't crack?

The fish motif appears throughout our home, as we are two happy-go-lucky Pisceans who feel lightly committed to our astrological sign. I took a page out of my father's book, and without describing the exact process (because there was none: I improvised as I went along), on two consecutive days (because it was too much fun to stop at one) I did not come up for air. The crick in my neck didn't stop me either. Besides, I had plenty of glass, crystals, beads, and baubles, all of which found their way into my wire mobiles. In the end, there was almost no distinguishable similarity between the Calder fish and mine except the idea, and now my "rainbow trout" and "chubfish" swing side by side, suspended by wire from hooks in the ceiling of our living room. There is hardly a person who enters the room who doesn't walk straight over to the pieces and ask where they came from, remarking on the sparkling "scales" that throw kaleidoscopic reflections on the walls as the sun makes its way across the sky.

In the past, whenever anyone suggested that I was lucky to have several means of expressing my creative impulses, I either felt defensive (that old jack-of-all-trades-master-of-none anxiety), or I feigned modesty, out of embarrassment, attributing my projects to an abundance of nervous energy. Secretly, I do feel very lucky to have these resources, and I am learning how to say "Thank you" and acknowledge my gratitude openly. In the case of the fish, I have been outrageously *im*modest, because it was not only a thoroughly enjoyable project, but it also yielded something I find beautiful and unique. In fact, it pleases me more than if I had given ten good concerts.

For me, the fish are not simply Piscean symbols; they are icons and reminders to follow my bliss, as Joseph Campbell advises, as I did those blissful afternoons on my screened porch, surrounded by wire, glass, and everything I could find that sparkled and shone.

Alfie

I HAD no more than a momentary twinge of nostalgia for my own youthful years of excitement and possibility while assisting Alfie in filling out the forms for the Young Artists Concerto Competition.

My most conscious thought was that I must be careful to address him as "Alf" from then on. I had ventured to mention at a recent lesson, "Alfie, now that you are sixteen, I don't think you ought to be using the name 'Alfie' any more for your professional life, and somehow I don't think 'Alfred' is suitable either. You'd have to be Brendel to use Alfred. Even though you are Italian, 'Alfredo' is too pretentious. What do you think of 'Alf'? It's sort of distinctive, different, catchy, isn't it?" Linked to his mellifluous surname, it made music.

He pondered it for only a few seconds and replied, "I like it! It feels like me!" And poof, we had a stage name.

The concerto competition required that Alfie submit a tape of both a Mozart concerto movement and a movement from another concerto of his own choice from memory.

"Why do I have to memorize it?" he had asked me.

"Well, that's a million-dollar question," I replied. "If you were a violinist, or a flutist, or even a harpsichordist, you probably wouldn't, but as you are a pianist, you do, and that's that."

"But *you* used music at your last concert, Ms. Montparker."

"Ah, yes I did. I can do whatever I want now," I said with a twinkle in my eye.

"How come?"

"Because I paid my dues, and played by memory for all those years since I was young, and now that I am older, I can do whatever I want! That's the nice thing about getting older: you can do whatever you want, and no one can challenge you! Besides I don't have time to memorize any longer, with the time I'm taking to teach you and the others, and writing about it!"

Then he came up with a very strange question. "You know, I just watched an old movie called *The Competition,* and the student says to the teacher, 'I have to get a tape ready to send in to this competition,' and the teacher says, 'Don't worry, I already did that for you.' Does that really happen? Would a teacher really make a tape and represent it as the student's playing? It's so dishonest and unfair!"

I told him that I doubted anyone ever does something that dishonest; but then I began to wonder about it. It surely would be easy enough to do, and certainly there was corruption all over the place—there's as much politics in the arts as anywhere else. I have heard tales of sexual politics, and deals made, and fixed results, and all sorts of discouraging things. One feels positively impotent faced with all those possibilities, but why should I disillusion him?

"Alfie. We are going to send in a tape of your playing that is so good, we don't have to worry whose teacher played what."

Alfie attends a Catholic parochial school, but we don't discuss his education or his religious beliefs at all. However, one day we engaged on several tangential points. I was trying to get him to express his feeling for the Mozart, to rejoice both physically and emotionally in the music. I asked him, "What would you say is the most important emotion in the world—the one that yields the most in return?"

"I don't know. Happiness?"

"No. What would Jesus have said?"

"Forgiveness?" he ventured.

"What about love?"

"Oh yeah," he responded readily, understanding immediately what I wanted.

"If you express your love for the music, your listeners will feel that love, and return it to you with love and appreciation."

He followed through with just the change I wished to hear. And then he brought up an altogether unrelated fact.

"You know what I hate?" he asked me.

"What?"

"Once a week we have Mass in school, and it's not just that I don't like the music, I absolutely hate it. I can't stand it!"

I knew exactly what he meant because during a trip to Italy, Ernest and I had toured the great churches, with their absolutely gorgeous acoustics, listening to choirs sing great music from Palestrina to the moderns. But the liturgical music of the services struck me as totally banal. The "hallelujahs" and ritual chants sung in masses, standardized in Catholic churches all over the world, have no greatness at all. Neither, in my opinion, does the Jewish liturgical music. Alongside the great requiems, passions, cantatas, and oratorios written for splendid occasions by Handel, Bach, Mendelssohn, Mozart, Schubert, and Verdi, everything else seems to pale. Even the little everyday things—such as the hymns or short motets by Thomas Tallis or William Byrd or Ralph Vaughan Williams, or the exquisite *Ave verum corpus* that Mozart wrote for the choir of the otherwise completely insignificant church of a small spa town his wife, Constanze, was staying in at the time—are so much better than the junk that replaced them. Alfie's lamentations and disappointments were proof to me of his instinctive musical taste.

I consider it one of my greatest privileges and challenges to be able to help elucidate what it is that makes a great composer great. With a student like Alfie, my own infectious enthusiasm when I demonstrate is instantaneously absorbed and soon manifest in his own playing.

Whenever I am about to play a passage for a student, if it's a work I have not played for a while, I might say, "Now I'm about to embarrass myself and sacrifice my vanity and pride to make a musical point to you." I throw ego to the winds to elucidate a gesture or a style, and no matter whether I come through it cleanly or not (whereupon I mumble "Whatever"), the good ones, like Alfie, invariably end up doing what I have asked of them. (Incidentally, no one but me is allowed to say "Whatever." I am the only one allowed to approximate something to make a point.) Alfie is always generous no matter how I think I have played.

"How come even when you haven't practiced it in many years, it always sounds so good when you play it?" I thanked him for the compliment, and the truth is that I do think I play well for my students, wanting to give them something memorable, and wanting so much for them to love the music. The second part of the truth, which may apply to the times I have to say "Whatever," is that I learned the fine art of faking from my late teacher, Leopold Mittman, but I usually acknowledge when I'm doing it with a wink or a grimace, just as Mr. Mittman did.

I live over a mile from the school bus stop, and when I can, I drive over and meet Alfie's bus; more often, he has to walk with a heavy backpack, and invariably he has his Walkman plugged into his ears with some new piano CD blasting into his head. After we chose the Rachmaninoff Second for his other concerto, Alfie got hold of a vast array of recordings of the work. ("I asked everyone to give me nothing but CDs for Christmas, but to ask me what I wanted first.")

To his credit, he is making many of his own artistic decisions; but certain matters of taste and propriety have come up. There were places I had to convince him that he did not have to be the fastest and the most dramatic pianist alive. Sometimes he challenged me, "Why *can't* I play this passage that fast? It says 'piu mosso.'"

"'Piu mosso' means more motion, not breakneck," I scolded.

"But everyone plays it fast!" he insisted.

In the end I told him that if he could play the passage in question entirely accurately and convince me that he had not sacrificed any of the musical content, I would accede to his tempo. Of course, I had to work hard to get him to take more time to breathe, especially in the trickiest places, instead of racing through and creating a train wreck. But in the end he proved himself, and I had to sit there and watch him amaze me. It reminded me of a moment when I was his age and brought to my teacher the monumental Brahms D Minor Concerto, which I wanted to study more than anything else. Mr. Mittman's initial response was to discourage me because of the huge demands of the score, my small hands, and my youth. But love is the greatest motivator, and I proved to my teacher, just as Alfie is proving to me, that when you love a work and are absolutely determined to learn it and play it, you will.

On the day of the recording session, Alfie arrived flushed from the walk from the bus stop and sat down at the piano to warm up while the audio technician connected his equipment. The competition committee required that the concerto movements be submitted without accompaniment. That meant that the piano part would be laid bare and exposed without any orchestral support, making the performance much more difficult, especially with the extra pressure of a live mike. (A microphone is much scarier than a live audience.)

Poor Alfie became nervous, having to repeat takes until he and I were both entirely satisfied, but exhausted.

"Why is it that I never feel that tapes ever represent my best playing?" he wailed.

"Because, Alfie, you have to be 200 percent prepared to get 90 percent under duress. And that's just a fact. None of us ever feel it goes as well as it does at home on our own instruments."

He was so weary and dispirited before the session was over that several times his lips and chin quivered with frustration and sadness, and my heart nearly broke. It was no good trying to tell him that this was what it would be like, that it's one of the hardest lives to live, that it has been likened to rocket science in terms of brain power and the Olympics in terms of physical energy, and that he had better steel himself to the rigors, because it won't get easier.

Not long afterward, Alfie stood patiently on the receiving line at one of my concerts, clutching two dozen roses, looking like the cat who ate the canary. When it was finally his turn in line, he blurted out a run-on sentence: "Ms. Montparker I loved your concert guess what I made the finals!" We squealed and hugged and danced around, and then we got serious, arranging several lessons in the week and a half ahead before the final auditions.

"I wonder who I'm up against."

I reminded him again, "You are up against *yourself*. We don't care who the others are. You have to worry about doing your *own* best, and communicating your love of the music, and then you'll do great. We won't even listen to the others, whoever they are. You'll go in there and play your heart out."

How well I knew the sensation of sitting in an audience and listening to another good pianist. Self-doubt reigns. Only at the keyboard do we remind ourselves, "This is what I do well. I know how to do this!" But it's difficult to keep the ego fired up, sitting idly by when others are playing well.

Two days before the finals, my phone rang after ten o'clock at night, when I was already in bed.

"Ms. Montparker?"

"Hi, Alfie."

"How do you know if you've practiced enough?"

"Honey, it's *never* going to feel like you have, and you almost never feel totally safe and cozy when you're away from the instrument, no matter *how* well prepared you are. It's the same for all of us. How much practicing did you do?"

"Over five hours today."

"Alfie! Go to sleep! Or do something nice for yourself. You'll be fine. It already sounded good last week at your lesson."

There was a silence and then he added, "I think I'm getting joint swelling. My fingers look a little puffy."

"Alfie, you know what you *are* getting?"

"No."

"You're getting to be a musical hypochondriac! Go to sleep! It's going to be great! We're going to have fun playing those concertos together."

"OK. Thanks. I needed you to tell me that."

He left me both chuckling and with my heart breaking for the tension he was experiencing.

The day before the finals, Alfie came for a final coaching of his two concerto movements, and before we played the Mozart, I said to him, "You know, I follow your opening eight bars of the last movement with the same eight bars in the orchestral tutti, and I'll be darned if I'm not going to play my best! You better open with all the love and joy in your heart, because I don't want to sound better than you, and I'm going to play my best!"

He countered by playing like a prince, and the movement went beautifully. But he said, "Why am I shaking? I'm trembling all over, Ms. Montparker."

I suggested, "You're very excited, Alfie. This is a big moment for you. Stand up and stretch. You'll be fine."

But a curious thing happened. Suddenly I began to shake in sync with Alfie, as though I were giving my own solo performance. True, I would be onstage accompanying him with those awkward unpianistic reductions of orchestral scores, not meant to be played publicly, and hoping that I would give him the support that he needed. That, in itself, might have been tension-producing; but I knew that the deepest source of my nerves was the vicarious anticipation, my hopes and prayers for him, and the simple rotten contagion of stage fright. I realized that I was doomed to feel those awful sensations, whether it be for myself or for my students. You simply cannot have the joys of the piano without the pains as well.

After the Mozart, we ran through the Rachmaninoff Second, which starts with a sequence of chords that begin pianissimo and grow into fortissimo. Discussions of dynamics are so much more effectual when considered qualitatively, rather than quantitatively. I suggested that instead of trying to increase, incrementally, from *pp* to *p* to *mp* to *mf* to *f* to *ff,* he think of the gradations of volume in terms of distance—-to picture these chords as emanating from Russian bells first heard pealing from afar and getting louder the closer he approached the source. Both the image of the enormous bells, "pulled by ropes" (as I described them), and a long conversation about the use of arm weight supporting his hands and fingers had a tremendous effect on his playing, which became positively heroic. We both felt mighty secure about the shape he was in, gave each other a hug and said we would meet the next evening early enough to try the pianos onstage.

No one I ever met wanted to be a pianist more than Alfie. I relinquished my resolution never to express a concrete opinion regarding a student's decision to make a career. Instead I decided early on to help him do it, with every bit of my energy and time, keeping him long past the designated lesson time and insisting that he come twice weekly, the second lesson gladly offered "on scholarship."

About two years into our work together, I told Alfie, after a particularly exhilarating lesson, "You know, I feel grateful and lucky that I am the one accompanying you on the journey across the bridge between student and artist."

His generous response was, "I feel the same way and I just said that to my mother on the way home last week."

A pianist-acquaintance of mine who was traveling too much to teach regularly sent this treasure of a student to me when Alfie was fourteen years of age. I knew he was gifted from the first meeting, but guiding the youth who was typing out notes, albeit with incredible speed and accuracy, to find his own spirit and voice and soul was one of my greatest challenges. I have felt this mission to be one of my greatest responsibilities. It wasn't easy to crack him open; I had to insist and cajole and poetize and mimic and demonstrate and flail my arms about and raise my voice and demonstrate some more until it all began to sink in; and then even his mother said one day, "You gave me chills, Alfie."

"I can't always give you chills when I play, Mom," he objected. Then he added, "I don't want you shivering throughout the whole piece!"

He thought that was funny, but I insisted in a serious tone, "Yes, you must! You must never again play without trying to move your listeners, and speak and sing the message in the music. Now that we see you can, we won't settle for anything less. Otherwise, don't play."

Since that day, with only a few setbacks and reminders, Alfie's playing has reflected the understanding that music is literature and that it speaks volumes, even more deeply than words.

I think I have never been more articulate or expressive than at his lessons. I search for the *mots justes* because he trusts me implicitly and does what I tell him so willingly and ably, and almost before all the words are out of my mouth. And I push him hard. When he complains that something is too difficult, I just stare blankly at him, and he manages to do it.

Before his very first competition, for which he had been exceedingly well prepared, he asked me, "What do I do if my foot starts shaking when I sit down to play?"

"Does that happen to you? I never saw that happen, Alfie."

"Yes, sometimes it shakes violently."

I gave him a lesson in breathing—a kind of calming yoga routine of deep breaths, imposing a beautiful image in his mind, counting down backward from twenty to one, relaxing his body from the toes up to his head, part by part; I wrote the whole method down in his notebook, instructing him to do it about a half-hour before he entered the room for his audition.

"And remember, I don't want you to listen to any of the other pianists. You just concentrate on your *own* work and do your *own* best, with no comparisons."

I was so touched by his trust when he phoned me excitedly from upstate: "Ms. Montparker, it worked! I did what you said with all the breathing and stuff. I got really calm, and I walked in and I wasn't nervous at all, and I played my best! I think I might have a chance!"

Later that day he phoned me again to tell me that out of thirty contestants he had received honorable mention, one of four awards, not bad for his first competition. He was learning from each experience, and further evidence of his trust came early in his preparation for another young artists' competition.

I was confronted with the dilemma of bringing up an issue that might have been too delicate for an adolescent boy to deal with. There was a certain part of his physical demeanor that was distracting and even unattractive onstage—after all, there is a physical aspect to any of the performing arts. Alfie's mouth had a way of dropping open when he was deep in concentration, and he appeared to be halfway between religious rapture and low mentality. This boy has brains to spare and the rare ability to focus no matter what is going on around him, which is something I was very hesitant to tamper with; if he had to divide his attention between the music and keeping his mouth closed, it might easily result in some mishap. But I decided to chance it and launched into a rather circuitous discussion of mannerisms in general. I told him that almost everyone has a little involuntary thing that occurs when deeply concentrating—a furrowed brow, grimaces, humming, mouthing the music, and in my own case, drawing in my cheek so that when I practice a lot, I develop a ridge along the inside of my mouth.

I told him that he was a very nice-looking person, but . . . and he saved me any further graphics by interrupting me with, "Oh, you mean my open mouth? My mother is always telling me that."

"Well," I responded, "it would be a pity to have that distraction. Why not try to reserve a little bit of your concentration and try to get out of that habit? If it detracts from the music, forget about it."

He was a remarkably good sport about it. The subject of mannerisms, whenever broached by an interviewer to any of the concert artists who manifest some rather grotesque cases, has been met with defensive and almost covetous protectiveness of their personal idiosyncrasies; they avow that they are not aware of any such characteristics, and that the whole matter is of little consequence. I agree that in the highest scheme of things, an individual physical characteristic is the last consideration when compared to the profound matters of getting to the essence of the music, much less getting through the rigors of a concert program. And that was my dilemma: I did not want to blow the issue out of proportion.

But Alfie, who is up for any challenge, whether musical or extra-musical, managed to dominate his old habit most of the time. In fact, a week later at a group workshop with the rest of my students, after playing his pieces he rose from the bench and ingenuously asked the group, "Did I keep my mouth shut?"

I gently suggested to him that he needn't make this part of his musical offering public, that it had been a private discussion between the two of us; but he was undaunted and innocent, free from any self-consciousness and willing to discuss it openly. I think that speaks not only to the informal and friendly atmosphere of our workshops and the generosity of my students as an exceptionally nice bunch of people, but to Alfie's receptive personality and his fervent intention to make a career. As it turned out, we all had a good tangential discussion on the visual aspects of performance that did everyone some good. But I should add that not long after these discussions, he resumed his old habit of allowing his mouth to drop open, and I decided never to bring it up again.

It is doubtful that Alfie's talent would have come to such early fruition had we all not ganged up on his father to buy him a fine piano. His parents are divorced, and it is clear he gets a lot of love from each of them. But the negotiations and delicate diplomacy about finances were very tricky, and at one point I phoned his dad, who months earlier had made the commitment to get a piano but now was dragging his feet about the final steps, and pulled out a double-barreled shotgun: I lectured and pleaded and explained what a handicap his son was laboring under, practicing on an instrument that could offer him nothing toward the development of a concept of beautiful tone, not to mention responsive action. I went beyond prudence expressing my belief that Alfie could have a major career (which no one can ever truly predict; there are too many variables, of which talent is only one). I went way out on a limb because nothing counted to me except the final realization of Alfie's dream.

When his father came through, and Alfie finally got the Steinway of his own choice delivered to his home, I relived a parallel moment in my own past. He didn't want to go anywhere; he abused his body practicing—he was like the ballerina who donned the red shoes and couldn't stop dancing. He couldn't believe it. He was too young to express certain profound life experiences that enrich one's playing, but now his passion began to flow from deep, untapped sources of love, gratitude, and unabashed joy.

It was thrilling to hear him describe those golden moments when the core of the music made itself known to him after hours of work—that sudden ray of light that illuminates the hitherto hidden meaning—-meanings that a teacher cannot tell a pupil. Alfie is finding these things out for himself. He is also finally developing a beautiful, complex tone, listening for overtones and a cantabile quality that he had little sense of earlier. His excitement is my excitement. He is one of my musical children.

On the other hand, there have been lessons when I feel I am yanking him up by the bootstraps. For the most part I have chosen his repertoire, but when he came to a lesson clasping the score of the Liszt B Minor Ballade in the Earl Wild edition, I tried to discourage him from studying it, for both technical and emotional reasons. However, he had fallen madly in love with the piece and would not be discouraged. A week later he had mastered the wretched left-hand chromatic passages as well as anyone, and in a short time he had learned the piece from memory. His technical prowess was awesome, but I had to keep stopping him to demonstrate expressive touches that were escaping his attention. Delicate phrases that he was playing softly enough were still missing a certain indescribable sweetness and fragility; other phrases ought to have been like world-weary sighs. He played the knuckle-busting octave passages as well as they can be played, but there was no fury, no grandiose gesture, no breathlessness. All of these musical messages take a lifetime to experience, and yet I felt compelled to try to compress time and communicate what was missing.

At one point, when he expressed fatigue and frustration, I chided him: "Alfie, anyone who hears you is going to think, 'At sixteen he shouldn't be playing this work. He doesn't have enough experience.' They don't know I tried to discourage you from playing it. But you were determined. And you *are* playing it after all, superbly well—technically. But not emotionally. So here I am pouring *my* passion into you, *my* sighs, *my* world-weariness, *my* love, *my* tenderness, all of which *must* be in this piece, or else don't play it! And when you leave tonight, I will be nothing but an empty vessel!"

These last words I uttered with mock exasperation, as a joke. But understanding how much of my energy had gone into that lesson, and having a lot of sweetness in him, he said, "Thank you," and I knew he meant it.

When the evening of the finals arrived, Alf and I stood outside in the hallway together, listening in spite of ourselves to the excellent performance of the Grieg and Beethoven "Emperor" Concertos, just before we were to enter the stage to play his two concerto movements. I was nervous both for myself and for him. He was playing better than I ever hoped he would, and I knew his chances were superb. I just prayed he would do his best. We made small talk, and Alfie kept asking strange questions to fill the time: "Are there any concertos that you know of that end softly?" (I couldn't think of any offhand.) "Why is late Liszt considered so great, when I find much of it so difficult to understand?"

I tried to explain the meditative qualities as reflective of the composer's years as an abbé, and mentioned the music's harmonic sophistication, bridging into the twentieth century. I talked about Liszt's alliance to Wagner, and when I mentioned the fact that Wagner married Cosima, Liszt's daughter, he looked shocked, and exclaimed, "I thought Liszt was a priest!"

"Later in his life, he became an abbé, but he had women swirling around him for all his younger years, because he was such an amazing virtuoso."

"No wonder I love to play Liszt!" he said with amusement.

"Do you want to be surrounded by women who admire your playing?"

"Why not?" he replied with a shrug and a huge grin.

How in the world this exchange was related to the Mozart-Rachmaninoff audition he was about to enter, I couldn't figure out. We were both obviously trying our best to assuage our nerves and amuse each other.

We got the signal to enter, and Alf looked sharp in his tux, bright-eyed, *simpatico*, confident, as we took our seats at the two Yamahas nestled onstage. The pianos were brand new, and during our warm-up time, we both had agreed that they sounded and felt superficial to us. Nevertheless, we adjusted, and Alfie played spectacularly well for 98 percent of his performance. Throughout the playing we made eye contact across both pianos and threw musical balls to each other, and any educated listener could hear how musically gifted he was. But he had two tiny lapses in concentration that had never occurred before; even so, his playing was so sensitive and beautiful that I felt hopeful as we left the stage. He was very worried about the mishaps, and I tried to tell him that they weren't consequential, despite my own private regrets.

He was the last of the three finalists to play, and the jury left the auditorium to make their decisions. For three-quarters of an hour we sat rigid with anticipation, and finally the announcement was made that Alfie had won second prize. I had to coach him to smile and prod him to go up and accept his sizable check and award without showing his disappointment. Earlier he had whispered that winning second prize would be the worst, because it would mean that he just missed winning first. In fact, that was exactly what had happened. I was told that the jury of four had been split two-two, and after long deliberations, the conductor finally broke the tie with his concerns about the slips Alfie had made.

I think I convinced him that there was an important lesson in every experience, and that he had long years ahead with many first prizes of his own to win. The primary message was that he had the talent and technical skills and needed to elevate his powers of concentration. His family and I showered him with verbal bouquets reflecting our pride and happiness for his success. He handled himself well enough, but he went home with a heartache.

Alfie also went home with a feeling of unrest that had a somewhat dark side for both of us. I believe he secretly wondered whether he ought to be studying at the Preparatory Division of the Juilliard School with a "big-name teacher" (as did the first-place finalist). Alfie's second prize included a cash award and a master class with a recent prizewinner of the prestigious Van Cliburn Competition, who gave him some suggestions and ideas about the Rachmaninoff concerto. He related to me at our next lesson how the pianist had spent almost the whole session on the first eight bars and asked, "How come we don't spend as much time on details as he did?"

His question stung me. I had to remind him of how we spent a half of a lesson on those very opening bars alone, how much material he is working on that has to be covered in our frustratingly short two-hour lessons, and how by the time he played the concerto for that coaching session, there was precious little *left* to be discussed, so that they had the luxury of zeroing in on small details. I heard a new competitive and political inflection to his thoughts, and as painful as it may have been for me to experience his doubts, and as painful as it will ultimately be to lose him, I was glad to know he has this aggressive and ambitious mentality. He will need it in the years ahead.

At the next lesson I asked him with mock self-pity, "When you are famous will you still remember me?"

"Are you kidding? You will always be my main teacher!" he exclaimed with utter sincerity. I almost cried.

In fact, he was headed to a summer program, Pianofest, where he would be thrown into a den of lions, where he would be coached by some "big-name" teachers, and where some of the finest young pianists around might easily, on the first day they all congregate, pull their tricks out of their respective hats—twenty Chopin études each, knocked off to impress the hell out of each other, trying to put each other on the defensive, like birds fanning out their plumage to intimidate their rivals. The program's pianist-director, Paul Schenly, laughed and told me, "If I hear them doing that, I have to run in and stop them, reminding them that that is not why they are here." Then he asked me whether I thought Alf would be able to handle that atmosphere, emotionally, since he would be the youngest, and I, in turn, asked Alfie at his next lesson whether he thought he could.

He was confident about the program, and I think I got him to understand that the best path he could take would be to stay focused on his own work; yes, keep aware of the demands and standards that are expected from him in all the programs and studies he would be undertaking in the years ahead, but stay clear of being sucked into rat races. I can only warn him; he will have to live it out for himself.

The atmosphere at Pianofest is actually quite collegial and mutually supportive. Alfie will form his first friendships with musical peers, one of the treasures of the profession. He will learn firsthand that he is only one of countless young talents, another important lesson. And he will learn to *listen*: for individuality, along with all the other criteria. It is a privileged milieu, and I am certain it will generate both excitement and anxiety.

For my part, that high-powered atmosphere will reinforce my assurance that I am content to be me, and not a young person starting out in music. I have traveled a good bit of my path, and he is just setting off on his. He is alternately innocent and enlightened, bushy-tailed and fearful. From where I sit, he seems to have a mighty good chance, but it's a long corridor with many doors.

Alfie came for a lesson just before he left for the Pianofest summer program. He played me his recital program, all memorized, in tip-top form. He had absorbed the Hungarian idiom for the Bartók Suite, Opus 14, had become a graceful Mozart player, and had developed a ravishing *jeu perlé* for the Chopin pieces. He finished the lesson with performances of Liszt's *La campanella* and the B Minor Ballade. By the time he finished, tears were streaming out of my eyes. To watch any young person so focused and involved with the music is moving; but here was someone I had nurtured musically for hours every week for several years who had undergone a metamorphosis from musical child to young artist, and we would still have one last year to work together before he would go off on his mission.

I listened and heard the relatively newfound poetry, the depth of tone, the nuances; I heard bits of myself, bits of my teacher, but mostly I heard Alfie. He had found his own voice.

Seeing how he had moved me, he said, "I don't just want to be a pianist. I want to be a great pianist."

"Alfie, I think you *will* be a great pianist."

"Thanks. I think I will, too." Then he added, "But I don't just want to be a great pianist. I want to be the defining pianist of the century, like Liszt was."

"Alfie, it's enough to want to be a great pianist."